WE ALL LIVE IN A PERRY GROVES WORLD

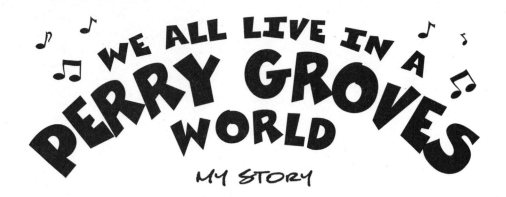

WE ALL LIVE IN A PERRY GROVES WORLD

MY STORY

PERRY GROVES

with John McShane

JOHN BLAKE

Published by John Blake Publishing Ltd,
3 Bramber Court, 2 Bramber Road,
London W14 9PB, England

www.blake.co.uk

First published in hardback in 2006

ISBN-13: 978 1 84454 319 9

British Library Cataloguing-in-Publication Data:

A catalogue record for this book is available from the British Library.

Design by www.envydesign.co.uk

Printed in Great Britain by Creative Print & Design, Ebbw Vale

3 5 7 9 10 8 6 4

Papers used by John Blake Publishing are natural, recyclable products
made from wood grown in sustainable forests. The manufacturing processes
conform to the environmental regulations of the country of origin.

All pictures from the author's collection.

To my sons Lewis and Drew: You can be anything
you want to be.

Acknowledgements

I will be forever grateful to my dad and mum: my dad for his total belief in me, and my mum for never judging me, no matter what. To Mandy, mother of my sons Lewis and Drew. To Mick Brown for getting me on the first rung of the ladder, to all my coaches good and bad (you can learn from both sorts), to George Graham for giving me the opportunity to play for Arsenal, my stepmum Dawn, sister Zoe and brothers Zac and Jordan. And to Judith and Kate.

Also to my beloved family: Ron and Sheila, Martin and Denise, Dave and Marina, Timothy and Sandy, Jamie, Ashley, Claudine and Sarah.

And to my friends: Chris (Chinney), Paul (Ginge), Deane (Big Nose), Pete (The Sicilian), John (Lenardo), Steve (Whit), Ray (Raymondo), Chris (Saskia), Mick (Pack), Pierre (Rocky), Pete (Quifford), Paul (Dugsy), Dave (Sumo) and Neil (Hammers). Good mates are priceless.

Finally, to my co-author John McShane for helping me recall the good, and some not-so-good, times in my life.

Prologue

It was 7 May 2006, and some of the greatest players ever to play for Arsenal were parading around Highbury, a ground we had all called home at some time in our lives.

The occasion was the 2,010th and last game played by the Gunners – or the Gooners as we all call the club – before everyone packed up and moved to their new home at the nearby Emirates Stadium. After the 4–2 victory over Wigan, more than 70 heroes who had pulled on that famous red and white shirt – players like Charlie George, Liam Brady and Ian Wright – were applauded by a crowd of 38,359. They were introduced as Legends – and I was one of them.

Yes me, Perry Groves. The red-haired 'Ginga' from Colchester United, the bloke with the Tintin haircut, who had been George Graham's first signing as he built an all-conquering side at the club, a dynasty carried on with flair by Arsene Wenger's Thierry Henry-led side. The same Perry Groves who had scored on his home debut and been loved by the fans – only to end up the target of the boo-boys in later years.

I'd been on winning and losing sides at Wembley, picked up two Championship medals, played at Lisbon's Stadium of Light in the European Cup, and taken part in one of the most famous games in British football history – Arsenal's last-gasp 'Fever Pitch' victory at Liverpool that clinched the league title against all odds.

I'd also been part of an Arsenal drinking club that could have seen off any opposition, been unfaithful throughout my marriage, fallen out with some of the most famous names in football and seen my career end through injury when I was only 28. Yet the fans still chant my name years after I finished playing, websites tell stories of my deeds and somehow or other, and much to my surprise, I have become a cult.

Let's make one thing clear: I don't call myself a 'legend' – just a man who was lucky enough to have memories to last a lifetime. The night Highbury closed for business after 93 years I ended up with my sons Lewis and Drew, and my partner Judith, recalling happy times with men I had played alongside – men like David Seaman, Kenny Sansom, Steve Bould and Wrighty. And just to show that nothing much changes really, once the family had gone I ended up in a West End nightclub with Bouldie and didn't get home until 5.20 the next morning. Just like the old days.

Let me cast my mind back to how it all began...

1

Let's start, as they say, at the beginning. I'm a Cockney, born at St Bartholomew's Hospital in London – known to everyone as Barts – on 19 April 1965, and brought up in Bow in the heart of the East End. Barts is a famous hospital, just down the road from St Paul's Cathedral and the Old Bailey, and being born there certainly gave me a better start in life than my dad had.

He's Arnold John Groves – 'Ginger' to his pals; I'll leave you to guess why – and he came into the world at an open prison in Epping in Essex. Before you jump to the wrong conclusions, it was March 1940 and Londoners had been evacuated because of the Blitz, so the prison was being used as a hospital. He later met my mother, Patricia Kathleen Healy, descended from a London-Irish family, at a local dance in the East End, and in the due course of time I came along.

I turned out to be an only child, so you'd think they could have made a better job of choosing a name for me. Mind you, although it's bad enough going through life with a name like Perry, it could have been a lot worse. My folks were big fans of the actor Pernell Roberts who played Adam in the popular cowboy series *Bonanza* on TV. They actually toyed with the idea of calling me Pernell for a while. 'Pernell Groves' – the very sound of it gives me a chill! Heaven forbid, but given their liking for the show they could have called me Little Joe or Hoss, two other characters in the series, so it could have been worse. Just.

Thankfully, they chose the lesser of the two 'P' evils and plumped for Perry, not Pernell. When I eventually started playing for Arsenal, *The Times* newspaper, no less, said my name sounded like the address of a cider company. Better that than Pernell Groves, though – fine for a cul-de-sac in Sidcup, not so good for a football star.

We had a family tradition of footballers. Dad's uncle, Vic Groves, played for Arsenal from 1955 to 1964 and captained them for a spell. He was the Gazza of his day – without the booze, drugs or tears, if you see what I mean – and even played for England at amateur and youth level. Great-uncle Vic was the first Groves to play in Europe, because he played for a London XI that took on Barcelona in the Inter-Cities Fairs Cup Final in 1958 in the days when it was one city (rather than one club) against another. European club competition was virtually unheard of then, but later it became the UEFA Cup.

Vic was part of a fine team at Highbury in the 1950s. Internationals like Dave Bowen, Jack Kelsey and Tommy Docherty were all in a good side who took some beating back in the days of the £20 maximum wage, proper short-back-and-sides haircuts and when the main group of 'foreigners' in a side inevitably came from Scotland.

Dad had two other uncles, called Reggie and Bunny Groves –

Bunny was the better player – and my father himself was an old-style bustling centre-forward, although he never played professionally.

By the time I came along, my parents were living in Monier Road in Bow, London E3, right in the heart of the East End. It was a two-up, two-down house, with a toilet out the back and a tin bath in front of the fire. No, I'm not making it up: I can just about remember being in that bath with the fire roaring away. This was a quarter of a century after Hitler had tried to destroy east London with his bombs, and 25 years before the yuppies moved in to finish the job by sending property prices through the roof. Monier Road is still there, but our house was demolished long ago to make way for a factory.

One of my first memories was of having a little 'Mr Rusty' tricycle that I would pedal around on. Back in those days I'd happily set off to the café down the road and someone would buy me a milkshake until Mum or Dad came to fetch me. They knew I'd either be in the café or at the grocers near by. Nowadays, there would probably be a full-scale air and sea search for a missing four-year-old, but, as the song goes, it was all so different then.

You might be thinking that I'm about to start one of those East End childhood sagas, but you're wrong. Things were about to change dramatically. Dad, who was working for URS as a lorry driver, decided he wanted to move out of London, so, when an opportunity for families to move to Suffolk as part of an overspill move came up, he went for it. We could have gone to Haverhill, but decided instead to move to Great Cornard about a mile from Sudbury, so close that some people think of it as a suburb.

It's not one of those twee chocolate-box villages but it's nice enough and, at the last count, had a population of around 8,000.

Our house, at 16 Hawthorne Road, had – luxury of luxuries – an inside toilet and bathroom and a coal bunker out the back. Many of the houses there were built around squares with a nice patch of grass in the middle, and we were among the first to move in. Pretty soon, the houses began to fill up, mainly with families from London – that or the occasional elderly couple.

School was the nearby Pot Kiln Primary and it was there that I learned at a very early age that I was different from most other children. Life can be tough for A Boy Named Sue, as Johnny Cash used to sing, but it can be pretty horrible for a boy with red hair too.

Like my dad before me, and quite a few others in our family, I was a carrot top. Describe it how you like – auburn, strawberry blonde, rusty – it doesn't make any difference, a ginga is a ginga is a ginga. The first thing to know is how to pronounce it. It's not with soft 'g's as in gingerbread, but with a hard 'g' at the start and in the middle, so that it rhymes with singer. I was a ginga then, I was during my playing career – from my mullet days to my trademark Tintin look – and I am now, although it's a little bit thinner on top.

Children always pick on someone who is different. In those days there were no ethnic minorities in Suffolk, so gingas were the minority and the kids would play 'get the ginger' because of my red hair. I never got beaten up, but they would take the piss out of me. It taught me at an early age that you have to be independent, believe me.

One of my earliest football memories is playing at the school under the eyes of the woman games teacher (who was actually called Miss Game), a spinster who looked about 98 but was in reality only 50-ish, when I was about six or seven. She would be dressed in her skirt and what looked to me like little slippers.

In one game, I didn't pass to this lad who was on my side who was absolutely useless and she asked me why. I've never been one to lie when put on the spot, so I told her the truth. 'He's crap,' I said. She stopped the game and said to me, 'Do you realise the upset a remark like that could have on other people?' I told her no, because I didn't. Then she made me pass the ball to him. It was a great lesson to learn. First it taught me that football is a team game – you can't do it all yourself. Second, it made me realise that it's not someone's fault if they are not as good as you are at something. As long as they try their best, there isn't much more they can do.

I loved football: I remember just wanting to play it all the time. Dad would take me to Great Cornard recreation ground, where we would play. Nothing too unusual in that, you might say – dads play football all the time with their lads, but it was different with mine. Most dads let their kids win. Well, not my dad. He was like Competitive Dad from *The Fast Show*. There was no letting the ball dribble through his legs on purpose and then pretending I was too good for him. We'd put some clothes down as goalposts and he'd go in goal and he never let me score if he could help it. He would dive all over the place to save my shots. You'd think we were at Wembley rather than on a little patch of grass in East Anglia – Gordon Banks, eat your heart out. If I was to score past Dad, it would have to be on merit. There were no charity goals on offer during my shoot-ins.

I don't know what a psychologist would make of that these days, and I don't care. All I know is that it made me a better player because I realised from a very early age that you have to fight for everything. I'm the same with my two sons Lewis and Drew now: they must earn everything.

I remember I had two balls – no jokes please – that I treasured.

There was an orange plastic 'Wembley Trophy' one and a proper white leather one that I used to carry in netting and clean after every game. Soon I started playing for a local team, the Cornard Dynamos, which was run by two men, Eddie Merton and Peter Thurlow. I was playing in their under-ten side by the time I was six. The problem was they wouldn't allow me to play in their league games because I was too young. It would have been a breach of league rules.

My best mate was a lad called Warren Brown and day after day, winter or summer, we'd play football together until it got dark. That's all I wanted to do. I was happy as long as I had a ball to kick around. Talk about football crazy.

When I wasn't playing football, I was watching it. It's not like it is now with virtually every major game shown live or in highlight form on one TV channel or another. Once you've finished with the Premier League or Champions League, it's easy to catch up with the latest results from Spain, Italy or wherever. But back in the early 1970s it was very different. A glimpse of top football then was as rare as dirt on George Graham's highly polished shoes would be a few years later.

So Saturdays were special for me. Mum and Dad would go to the pub, the Maldon Grey, with their pals Mick and June Brown and I'd stay in with Prince, our springer spaniel, for company and watch television all night. I can remember the programmes even now: detective shows like *Cannon* or *Starsky and Hutch* – followed by the highlight of the week, *Match of the Day* with David Coleman and Jimmy Hill.

They always seemed to be showing Leeds United, Liverpool or Sheffield United who had, for one of the few times in their history, a decent side with a genuine class act in an English international called Tony Currie. He looked like a pop star with his flowing, long blond hair, and I loved the way he played, especially his 'foot-overs' where he'd put his foot around the ball which was practically revolutionary in 1972. I'd try to do it myself outside our house and practically broke my leg!

It was bliss watching those Division One – as it was then – games. They wouldn't show all the matches, because they weren't allowed to, so I, like football fans all over the country, made the best of what we got.

After the football had finished, I'd stay watching the box and the night's viewing would end with the *Michael Parkinson Show*. Mum and Dad might still be down the pub having 'afters', so I'd stay glued to the set and when the dot eventually came on as TV closed down for the night it would all be quiet – and I'd shit myself with fear. These days, social services would be breaking the front door down, but I was as safe as houses and I loved it, the fear and all.

About this time, I had to make a big choice – whether to support Manchester United or Arsenal. Now you might think it was a foregone conclusion that I would plump for Arsenal, but it was a close thing for a time – well, I was only seven. My great-uncle had played for Arsenal, Dad was a 'Gooner' through and through, and most of the men in the family were Arsenal supporters. But I've always been one to look in the mirror when I am passing and I liked the look of the Manchester United away strip of the time – white shirts and black shorts – and I could just picture myself wearing that in years to come. So for a while I guess I supported them both, strange as it sounds now. I could even have ended up supporting United – perish the thought! Fortunately, I was saved, but I'll tell you about that a little later.

Life was OK in Great Cornard, and for holidays the family would go in force to Ladbrokes Holiday Camp at Caister, near

Great Yarmouth. We'd spend a week there – Mum, Dad and me, Uncle Ron and Auntie Sheila, cousins Marina and Denise, and Nan and Granddad, Tim and Doll. We'd have three or four chalets for the family, and me and Dad would play sport all week. Marvellous.

They always had a dads' game for the fathers and he loved to take part in that. He was unbelievably competitive and wanted to win, although at least he was a team player. At that age, I was all 'me, me, me'.

My first game in proper kit for the Dynamos came when I was about seven. We played at Wells Hall Primary School and we ran out in the old Birmingham City blue and white strip. Dad bought me some shin pads and a pair of black with yellow stripes Adidas boots, 'Franz Beckenbauer Supers', for about £14 – and four or five different sets of screw-in studs. I always fancied myself as an inside-forward, but I was the youngest player on the pitch so they put me on the right wing.

Life with the Dynamos gave me an early taste of the highs and lows of football. We were losing one game 8–0, all the other players were bigger than me and I'd seen so little of the ball standing out there on the wing I might as well have been the linesman. (Some things never change!) Then, miracle of miracles, someone actually gave me the ball. I woke up just in time to control it and sent in a cross that the goalkeeper came out to collect. He missed it, the ball hit a mound, bounced and went in the net.

I didn't know what to do. I was overjoyed. Dad was on the touchline and had seen my first goal. I felt so happy I started to cry. It was that feeling of elation, just to touch the ball and then score... it was an indescribable emotion. Let's put it this way – I never felt like that again until I started shagging. Yes, it was as good as that.

We ended up losing the game 10–1, but I didn't care. I was just happy that I'd scored. Weird as it might sound, that attitude stayed with me throughout my career. Yes, there were times when you ended up on the losing side and you felt sorry for yourself and disappointed for the team and fans. But the main thing I cared about after every game was how well I had played. If you ask other professionals if they feel the same, a few of them – the honest ones – will tell you they do. The bullshitters will tell you the opposite.

From that day on, I had an ambition – I wanted to be on *Match of the Day*, I wanted to play football full time. It was nothing to do with the prospect of earning big money as a professional footballer – that wasn't even a consideration for me. It was simply that the thought of it was the most exciting thing in my young mind.

The next season I started to play regularly in the Dynamos' under-ten side, usually against lads two or three years older than me, and I played for them for three years. Once we had three lads – Tony Jupp, Andy Scott and Eddie Doyle – selected for the league side, which was made up from the best players in the league. Although I was younger than them and they were our three best players, I was still disappointedly looking for my name on the board when it was announced they had been selected – I just wanted to be in the representative team.

Still, I would have a taste of the glamour side of the game and television coverage pretty soon – but not quite in the way I had dreamed of. We had a girl called Dawn Lawrence, who was eight or nine, playing for the Dynamos on the left wing and it got in the newspapers – a girl playing in a boys' side was a good story in those days. There was a lot of fuss about how she would have to change in a dressing room by herself before all the boys did and all that nonsense.

The next thing we knew Anglia TV had heard about it and came out to cover it – film crew, reporter, cameras, microphones, the lot. They wanted to film Dawn – who was a pretty good player as it happened – going past a couple of boy players, so me and my mate Warren Brown volunteered like a shot. A chance of early fame beckoned – and we blew it. Because when it came to the crunch we couldn't do it. We couldn't let her make us look stupid – you can't blame us. On the first three or four 'takes' in front of the camera, Warren brought her down – he wasn't going to let her pass, and I did the same.

This , of course, was exactly what the TV people did not want. They wanted her to fly past the boys, leaving a trail of pathetic lads in her wake. In the end, we failed the audition, so to speak, and they told us to move away while they chose some slightly more co-operative youngsters to be their stooges. Warren and I walked off in disgust. What a way to learn that what goes on in telly isn't for real!

Warren figured pretty large in my life at that time, but he managed to do what best mates shouldn't – he broke my leg! I was about eight and, as usual, playing on the recreation ground with Warren in goal and we just crossed shins and collided. I said, 'My left shin hurts', and Warren's dad had to carry me home. The shin ached all night and the next day Dad took me to hospital and they discovered a fractured fibula – I'd broken my leg! They put it in plaster for six weeks, although after four I was bored stiff and took it off. Looking back, that could have changed my life and been disastrous for English football if it had had a long-term effect. Thankfully it didn't. Thankfully for me, that is – others might think differently.

Soon I moved up to Great Cornard Middle School, playing either centre-half or central midfield. I know, me as a centre-half! It might sound strange but there was method in it as I could actually head the ball, which lots of kids can't, so it seemed a natural position for me. Anyway, we had a trial for the school team one Tuesday and the side was announced on the Thursday. Those two days seemed to last six weeks, and when the sheet went up all the lads at school were crowding around to see who would be in it.

Well, I was selected, but I still wasn't happy. I went up to the sports master, Dave Hinchcliffe, and – remember I was only nine – said, 'How come I'm not the captain?' Clever Mr Hinchcliffe must have been taken aback, but he calmly replied, 'I want you to concentrate on your game.' Good answer – but I still reckon it was bollocks. I was to hear similar rubbish from managers over the years, I can tell you. I wonder if George Graham ever met Mr Hinchcliffe.

Our headmaster was a man called John Budd, and there's only one word to describe him: fantastic. Like all headmasters appear to very small boys, he seemed ancient, 60 or 70, but he was probably only in his forties.

I don't know if you've ever seen the film *Kes*, but there is a wonderful scene in it with the late Brian Glover playing a soccer-mad teacher who imagines himself as Bobby Charlton in his pomp as he ploughs through the mud against a posse of bedraggled boys. Mr Budd – I can still hear the 'click click' of his metal-heeled shoes coming down the school corridor and his voice booming out, 'Boy! Boy!' – was like that.

There was an annual teachers' cricket match at school and it was almost part of the tradition that he would hit 50 and then retire. Unfortunately, one year another teacher, Pete Summers, who was umpiring, had different ideas and told the bowler just to bowl straight at the headmaster. One ball duly hit the headmaster on the pads and Mr Budd was given out lbw.

There's a cricketing story of the famous batsman WG Grace once disputing an lbw decision of 'out' by telling the umpire that the crowd had come to see him bat, not to watch the umpire go about his work. Well, this was Mr Budd's WG Grace moment.

'Are you sure?' he asked.

'Yes,' came the reply.

Talk about who blinks first. Being headmaster – well, it just wasn't cricket to dispute a decision, but he definitely didn't want to leave the crease. Eventually, he got as near to rebellion as the situation would allow and he asked the umpire, 'Would you like to reconsider?'

Back came the reply: 'No, sir.'

So off trooped the headmaster, and Pete Summers and us players were pissing ourselves. I can't help but feel that Mr Summers had another job lined up, otherwise his decision would have fallen into the 'bad career move' category.

On another occasion, Mr Budd was playing football with the boys and awarded himself a penalty. He gave it a good old whack – and the goalkeeper saved it. Not to be outwitted, the head swapped places with me at half-time so he was now playing for the winning team. Good move, Boss.

You might think from all this he was a bit of an ogre but nothing could be further from the truth. I have nothing but respect for him, even though he once gave me a slippering – and I hadn't done anything wrong! There was a fight in the dinner queue and the two boys involved – Paul 'Ginge' Robey and Chris 'Chinney' Heard, my best mates to this day – said it was my fault. Thanks, lads. 'Groves boy,' said Mr Budd, 'You are going to be punished.'

He had a collection of slip-on rubber plimsolls and he would match the size of slipper to the size of a boy's feet, so small boys received a small slipper hit while big lads got the big whack. I was a size six but said I was a four just to get a smaller slipper. I can still see him bending that slipper double in preparation for the whack he gave me. The other two boys went back to the dinner hall without being hit and I went back into the room, my arse still smarting, all on my own. Talk about life not being fair.

Then I heard Mr Budd enter the hall and saying to the women who were serving the food, 'Good afternoon, ladies. See Groves here – give him two "afters". Now that is what I call brilliant man-management.

Round about this time, my football week consisted of playing for the school on Saturday mornings and after school on Thursdays. Saturday afternoons I'd be watching Sudbury Town and Sunday morning I was playing for the Dynamos. That only left Sunday afternoons free, but I was usually watching the football on ITV, invariably with Gerry Harrison commentating. It was a regional programme, which was all right if you lived in the North West – you'd have Liverpool, Everton, Manchester United and City week after week. In Great Cornard, we got Anglia TV and that meant we got Ipswich, Norwich or Luton! Mind you, Ipswich were a half-decent team then.

I'd been to see my first 'proper' match at Sudbury when I was about eight – 'proper' in the sense that they had floodlights, nets and a referee in black. But at ten I went with a friend and his father to see Ipswich play at their Portman Road ground and, strangely enough, the opposition was Arsenal.

I recall that Arsenal had Terry Mancini at centre-half, a pretty good player but noticeable in that era for his shiny bald head at a time when most other players looked as though they were bass players in rock bands with their long hairstyles. Ipswich had a fair few internationals in their side that day, players of the calibre of Colin Viljoen, Mick Lambert, Mick Mills, Allan Hunter and Trevor Whymark.

I just loved it. Here I was watching in person players I had only seen on television before. They were no longer in a different universe, only to be seen thanks to the goggle box. There they were right in front of me, shouting and swearing away and clattering into each other with a force that you never realise when you are watching at home. I thought Sudbury Town had been good, but this...

When I was about 11, we moved from our council house to our own home in Great Cornard at, wait for it, Highbury Way. It was football all the time, and all my mates like Dave Bowes, Chris Heard, Paul Robey and Deane Potter lived within a few hundred yards.

I've mentioned my broken leg, and, as if that hadn't been bad enough, I came down with terrible knee pains when I was about 13 and now at the Upper School. It turned out I'd got Osgood-Schlatters disease, a pain that can affect adolescent lads because of too much sport, and I ended up having electric pulses pumped through my knee joints and no sport for six months. Six months!

Naturally, I got bored and really pissed off. Eventually, as a compromise, I ended up playing wicketkeeper at school cricket so that I could at least take part in some sport without hardly having to run. By the time it all cleared up, I had to make a sporting decision that was to change my life.

There's no point in being modest: I was good at most sports and I got into the school rugby team. I was fly-half for my own age group and on the wing for the Under-18s. I've always said that not all rugby players can play football, but all football players can play rugby – if they're brave enough. I now had to decide which sport I'd play. In those days, rugby was amateur, so you couldn't make a living out of it, so rugby's loss became football's gain. Or perhaps it was the other way round...

2

When I say that all I thought about was football, I'm not being totally accurate. Boys will be boys and I was aware that there might be other things – well, one other thing – in life. Dad had told me not to bother with girls and even in my early teens they would be around, or in your ear at dinnertimes, so I'd tell them, 'Get lost, I'm playing football!' Well, I always was a romantic.

But I do remember there was a nice girl called Jane Moorcraft when I was about 13. I could tell she was interested, so I came up with a great chat-up line, one that you don't hear every day of the week. 'Would you like to be a goalpost?' I said to her. It must have had the desired effect, because she said yes, so we had a kickaround with her as one of the posts. All was going well and could have been the start of a great romance – until I sent a shot her way. Instead of leaning outwards so the ball went past her into the goal, she leaned inwards and the ball went past her on the outside. It meant I hadn't scored. 'If you can't concentrate and be a post then piss off,' I told her. End of any prospect of teenage romance. Well, a man has to get his priorities right.

There was another girl in Great Cornard called Sarah Heath, but that didn't progress much either as she refused to take me round to meet her parents because I was a ginga. Good job I was thick-skinned – corn-beef-skinned might be a better description.

I've already mentioned I had a soft spot for both Arsenal and Manchester United – well, a few weeks after my 14th birthday, the teams met in the 1979 Cup Final. They were two fine sides who walked out that glorious sunlit Wembley afternoon and, on as perfect a surface as any footballer could wish for, managed to achieve what many had done before them – give the watching nation a pretty boring match to bring the curtain down on the season. Thanks to Brian Talbot and Frank Stapleton, Arsenal seemed to be coasting to an unremarkable victory with a secure 2–0 lead with just five minutes left. Then United came up with two goals in the blink of an eye from Gordon McQueen and Sammy McIlroy, and suddenly we had a cliffhanger.

But, not to be outdone, Liam Brady wove a little bit of magic down the left from the restart and the ball eventually came into the United penalty area from Graham Rix. Gary Bailey in their goal came out, waved at it like Superman and Alan Sunderland slid in to make it 3–2, writing himself into Arsenal legend in the process. Job done – I was a Gooner from that day on.

While we're on the subject of Wembley, I should mention my appearance there when I was just 15. I'd love to say it was for England Schoolboys or something equally prestigious, but I'd got into the Suffolk Schoolboys side by then and we were chosen to be ball-boys at the 100th Cup Final in 1980. Not only that, it was the Gooners again, for a record third consecutive Wembley appearance, and they were playing underdogs West Ham. I remember walking out behind the teams with 100,000 fans cheering and somehow thinking, All this noise is for me. Ridiculous, I know, but that's how it seemed.

I was put behind the goal at the tunnel end, and that was a lot of ground to cover at Wembley, I can tell you. There was me and another lad behind all the cameramen on the sand and running track. Once the ball came between the two of us and I started to fight with the other boy to get the ball. After a while, I heard an Irish voice shouting, 'Any danger...?' It was Pat Jennings, one of the greatest goalkeepers in Arsenal's history, and he – along with the rest of the players, a stadium full of fans and millions on TV around the world – were being kept waiting while me and this other lad decided who would get the ball. Eventually, I won and threw it back to Big Pat. Wish I hadn't. The Hammers caused an upset and beat us by that rarest of goals, a header from Trevor Brooking.

Afterwards, we were all given England-style shorts. Most boys would have been pleased with that, but when I got home I decided to tell everyone that mine had been worn by Trevor Francis, who was a massive star in those days. Well, why not?

By the time I was 14, I was in the West Suffolk Boys team. Mick Brown, who ran the Dynamos and was a massive help and encouragement to me and many other players over the years, started to write to clubs in the area to try to get me a trial. A local lad called Andy Lovelace had played for the Dynamos and had been taken on as an apprentice at Colchester, so there was an 'in' there. I also noticed that all the girls were hanging around him and thought, That's what I want to be like.

So Mick – who was my pal Warren's dad – wrote to Colchester, Norwich, Ipswich, Peterborough, Luton and Wolverhampton

Wanderers. I had a couple of games at Colchester, and then Wolves said they would like a look at me.

My dad had hardly ever missed a game I was in, either for the school, the Dynamos or a representative side, so he was made up about it all. We got up at 6am and he took me to Sudbury and put me, clutching my little drink and some sandwiches, on the train. I went by myself to Liverpool Street, across London in a taxi and then from Euston to Wolverhampton. I was crapping myself up on the train to the Midlands but eased the tension in the same way as generations of schoolboys had done before me – by reading copies of the girlie magazines *Parade* and *Knave* that I'd bought at Euston. I hid them inside a copy of the *Sun*, which I pretended to read during the journey, as you do.

Wolves were in the top flight then. They won the League Cup that year (1980) by beating Nottingham Forest and they had some famous players in their line-up. Emlyn 'Crazy Horse' Hughes, who was nearing the end of a fabulous career that had seen him become a Liverpool legend and an England regular, was there and they had recently signed Andy Gray for a then record £1.5 million from Aston Villa. These days Gray is known as a commentator on television, but he was then a brave centre-forward who scored goals wherever he went.

I was met at the station by an old boy called Joe Gardiner who took me to their Molineux ground where I met the youth-team manager, John Jarman. I spent a few days in the Connaught Hotel paid for by Wolves and trained with the associate schoolboys. Most of them were from the Midlands and they looked on me as an outsider turning up to take their jobs. Well, they were right there.

When I played against them, I remember wondering, How good am I really? and, although I was nervous to start with, I soon felt comfortable. It was exciting and frightening at the same time. I was up there for three or four days, eating at the club's training ground after training and then taken back to the hotel by coach.

Soon after I returned home, I got a letter offering me associate schoolboy forms at Wolves – the first step on the ladder! Suddenly I could say, 'I'm Perry Groves – I play for Wolves.' I signed, of course, and that meant I couldn't sign or have a trial with anyone else – as if I would. So for about 18 months I was an associate schoolboy with them, travelling up during school holidays and the like.

Then, in the summer of 1981, a letter dropped on our doorstep from Wolverhampton. The first line read, 'Dear Perry, We are sorry...' My heart sank. They said that, due to financial cutbacks, they were going to have to concentrate on local boys, and they weren't going to keep me on. Bollocks – it meant I wasn't good enough. It was from John Jarman, so it really was a 'Dear John' letter dumping me.

I was devastated – my world had fallen apart. I'd left school without any O levels – football was all I cared about – and now this. I was thinking I'd let my dad down but he, as usual, played a blinder. 'How bad do you want to be a footballer?' he asked. 'It's one man's opinion and there are 92 clubs out there. I know you are good enough.' Dad had 100 per cent faith in me and that, and his not worrying about it, gave me confidence.

But there I was at home at 16 with no job, while all my mates had started apprenticeships and the like. I managed to get a couple of weeks labouring that summer on the bridge that was being built over the River Orwell to take traffic away from Ipswich and that paid me £12 a day, and I tried to keep fit by running everywhere I went. I must have looked strange to everyone else as I zipped around the fields, but it wasn't the funniest of times.

But Mick Brown of the Dynamos got on the typewriter again on my behalf and wrote to Peterborough, Luton, Norwich, Ipswich and Colchester to see if they would have a look at me. Some of the clubs were having end-of-season trials. 'Take the first one that comes along,' Dad said. Don't worry, I was going to.

I had a run-out at Norwich and thought I did reasonably well. I went to Luton and changed in the back of Dad's lorry before the game. They said they'd get back to me, but I'm still waiting. Then I got a game with Peterborough's youth team against Tottenham Hotspur at their training ground at Chigwell in Essex. I was the best player on the park. I was fantastic, and we were beating them 3–0. We were giving them such a hammering that Spurs brought their A team on against us, but we still beat them 3–1.

Afterwards came the news I had been praying for. The Peterborough youth-team manager Graham Scarfe said, 'Come in on Wednesday and we'll sign you as an apprentice.' It was looking good – too good, as it turned out.

I got a call at home on the Monday asking me to come in on the Wednesday and play for the reserves as the manager Peter Morris wanted to have a look at me. The game would be against another reserve team but that didn't worry me. My dad had made sure I'd played for Long Melford when I was 15 to toughen me up against grown men, so I wasn't bothered at all by playing against professionals. I should have guessed it wouldn't be as easy as that.

I turned up on the Wednesday and found the others there were about 23. I was playing in midfield alongside a lad called Tim – and he was useless. Well, what do you expect? Have you ever heard of a half-decent footballer called Tim? The two don't go together, do they? 'Tim' and 'good player'. See, they just don't sound right. He didn't give me a pass all game. Perhaps he didn't want to – more likely he simply couldn't.

After the match, Graham Scarfe came up to my dad and asked him to come into the office. Once we were all seated comfortably, Peter Morris said, 'We're not going to sign you. You are no better than what we've already got.' Talk about hearing the proverbial pin drop.

Dad said, 'Say that again?'

Peter Morris replied, 'He ain't got it – he's not good enough.'

I've always reckoned I was pretty nippy on the pitch, and there and then in that manager's office I saw where I'd got my speed from. Dad was across the desk in the blink of an eye and grabbed Morris around the throat. Graham Scarfe leaped across to separate them. Oh dear. I looked on as my father struggled with this man who'd told me to take a hike, and I could see there wasn't a great future ahead of me at Peterborough. Having your dad get in a punch-up with your prospective boss was the River Kwai of bridge-burning.

Outside, Graham Scarfe said to us he might be able to get me back at some stage, but Dad said no. We were back to square one. But, as they say, the darkest hour is just before dawn.

Mick Brown had got in touch with Roy Massey, a local schoolteacher who had an excellent knowledge of local youth-team players. Roy must know his onions, because these days he's in charge of looking after under-16 youngsters at Arsenal. Anyway, he arranged for me to have some pre-season games at Colchester United. I played a game with the reserves at West Bergholt and scored, and then at Clacton Town and scored twice. I think I beat five men for one of them or perhaps it was just their fat centre-half – the memory can play tricks, you know.

Then I played in the FA Youth Cup under floodlights and we won 5–2 and I scored twice again. Was I on fire or what? The Colchester manager Bobby Roberts was at the game and said to the four full-time apprentices, 'You four have been embarrassed by someone who is not even full-time.' It's great to hear something like that, of course, but the other four were probably thinking, You flash bastard, and wanting to beat me up.

At the end of the game they signed me on a two-year apprentice's contract. There and then. Told you it was a funny game. And what riches awaited me. Well, £17 a week to be precise, rising to £20 in the second year. Oh yes, and a £6 win bonus on top. Look out, world! I was on my way.

3

Wow I'd hit the big time, I opened a bank account as we were paid every Friday. My best pal Chris 'Chinney' Heard was on £30 a week as a trainee supermarket manager, Paul 'Ginge' Robey was an apprentice carpenter on £27 and Deane 'Big Nose' Potter was on £25 working in the office of a DIY company. They all thought I was on a bundle, but in fact I was on a basic of £17 a week. I never talked about what I was earning. I was English, after all, and we don't do that sort of thing, do we? Plus, I wasn't all that keen on them knowing how small my pay packet was. I was happy for all my mates – and especially the girls – to think I was Billy Bigshot.

So, what was life like for yours truly at Colchester United? Well, I was 16 and there were four other apprentices about my age there. The most senior one got the best job – looking after the laundry – and that was dead easy. The next two had the home and away dressing rooms to keep clean and tidy. The fourth had the main stand to look after – and that didn't take long there, I can tell you. Then came the worst job of all – boot boy. You can guess who got that job, can't you?

I had 22 players' boots to clean and, as they had two pairs each, that meant 44 pairs of boots, week in week out. I practically died from Cherry Blossom poisoning. On Mondays, I'd be in at 8 or 8.30am, and the theory was that, to get match boots ready, you had to do them three days before the game. You were meant to put old newspaper inside to help them dry and keep their shape, but of course I couldn't be arsed. I never did it. I'd often be doing the boots a couple of hours before kick-off on match days.

You had to scrub them clean, then apply Dubbin – the wax that keeps football boots supple – and then make sure they went back in the correct numbered boxes so everyone knew where their boots were. It goes without saying that I would get that wrong a lot of times.

There was an old kit man at Colchester called Albert Danzy, whose claim to fame was that when he was a lad he'd gone out with Prime Minister Margaret Thatcher when she was just a grocer's daughter from Grantham. Whether he had or not I don't know – perhaps he was having us on or fantasising – but it was a strange thought that this old geezer might have had his evil way with the young Margaret Roberts (as she was then). At this time she was leading the country against the Argentineans in the Falklands crisis, and here was this old boy hinting he'd been out with her. I wonder if she was a goer. At least it would have shut her up for a while.

I got my first taste of publicity when a local paper took a picture of me cleaning the terraces with an old yard brush just after I'd signed as an apprentice. It made quite a decent show –

well, not all that much happened in Colchester – and they asked me for a few words to go with it. So I said, 'I've always wanted to be a professional footballer and now I'm aiming to be in the first team by Christmas.'

Nothing wrong with that, you might think, but the senior pros hated it. They thought, Who does this cocky ginger twat think he is? He's only been here five minutes and he's talking about the first team already. But I could sense the manager Bobby Roberts rated me and so did the first-team coach Ray Bunkell, so I didn't give a monkey's.

So when it came to the chores I was nowhere to be seen: I was always messing around with a ball somewhere. I just wanted to play. I'd hear them calling out, 'Where is that ginger-haired twat?' and I would just carry on out of sight playing with a ball.

Eventually, of course, I was called in to see the Boss in his office.

Roberts was a Scotsman from Edinburgh and he'd had a good career with Leicester in the 1960s, playing over 200 games alongside terrific players like Gordon Banks and Frank McLintock in one of the best sides Leicester ever had.

These meetings with managers in their offices were to become pretty regular throughout my career, and this one was pretty much on par with the ones that lay ahead.

'Sit down, son,' he said to me. 'Reports are getting back to me that you are not doing your job.'

I was only 16 and he was in his forties and my first manager, but I never was backward in coming forward, as they say. I told him, 'To be honest, I'm here to play football and practise, not to become the world's best boot boy.'

I was ready for a long debate on the subject – one of those in-depth chats that make life worthwhile – but I didn't get it. 'Do your job first, son, Roberts replied. 'If you have time, then play with the ball. You're fined £2.' Crikey, talk about short and sweet! It was the first time I had been fined by a club – but it wasn't going to be the last.

Colchester United – known to the handful of people who supported them as the 'U's – were in the old Fourth Division then. We often played our first-team home games on Friday nights so they didn't clash with other 'big' clubs in the area or down in London, but even so the average gate was only around the 2,000 mark. And when it comes to listing Great Football Stadiums of the World, their Layer Road ground certainly won't be there. The showers ran out of hot water after about 15 minutes, so, when there was no one about, I always tried to head for the referee's shower as it stood a better chance of providing hot water.

At this time, I was living at home with Mum and Dad, and getting on the 6.30am bus, which took one and a half hours to get to the ground for my morning starts. This meant I would often spend three hours a day travelling, so one day Dad said, 'We'd better find you some digs.'

'But, Dad,' I said, 'we only live 15 miles down the road.'

He just said, 'No – time to grow up.'

When the other apprentices, who all lived locally, heard I was going into digs, they thought it was hilarious.

And so I came to move in with the groundsman Tom Cheeney and his wife Margaret in their three-bedroom house in Prettygate, Colchester. Dad met them both and I think the club paid them about £15 a week for the privilege of having me under their roof. At least I had my own room with a portable black-and-white TV.

Now you'd think that being near the ground would mean that getting there every day would be no problem. I mean, that was why I had moved into digs in the first place. But nothing was that simple. The ground was about one and a half miles away and I was supposed to be in at 8.30am while Tom had to be in half an hour later.

At breakfast – Tom always had a boiled egg, never anything different – I would say to him, 'What time are you going in?' Tom had a Ford Escort Mk1 and it wouldn't have been any skin off his nose to give me a lift in. He would always say, 'I don't know,' and carry on eating his boiled egg. So I would think, Bollocks to this, and decide to walk to the ground. I couldn't take a chance on being late.

I told my dad about this so he bought me a baker's bike for £5 from Bury St Edmunds market and said, 'No excuses to be late now.' I used to leave the digs at 8.15 and battle through the wind, rain, sleet and snow, and time after time as I got to the ground there would be Tom pulling up in his car giving me a cheerful wave. I would think, You no-good, senile, old... He could easily have given me a lift – I'm sure he did it to wind me up.

This went on for three or four months until a chance came along for me to get my own back. Tom was a diabetic so he had to keep an eye on his blood-sugar levels. One day he was forking the pitch when I heard someone yell, 'Bloody hell!' I turned around and Tom had just keeled over. He was lying there on the turf, flat out.

Old Albert the kit man came out and barked at me, 'He needs a cup of tea – loads of sugar!' So I walked over to the groundsman's shed – I wasn't in too great a hurry – and eventually made him a mug of tea, filling it with six or seven sugars. Then I walked back to where a group of staff were gathered around Tom. As I got to him with the lifesaving cuppa, I thought, I'll make you suffer for not giving me a lift, and deliberately dropped the tea, making it look like an accident, of course.

Albert just looked at me and said, 'I hope my life never depends on you.' Then they got someone else to make him another cup. Should have done that in the first place, shouldn't they? It wasn't a nice thing to do, but I was very young – and the old bastard should have given me a lift anyway.

At this stage, I'd better point out that throughout my career I managed to laugh not only at my own misfortune, but also when other people ended up in the mire. Now this doesn't make me an evil person, just an honest one. I'm only human and, whenever something terrible happens to someone else, there is a part of all of us that thinks, Thank God that's not me, and almost enjoys their pain or discomfort. The vast majority of people pretend this isn't so – or at least try to hide their feelings – but I don't. It really is as simple as that.

So, that got even with Tom, but it left his wife to take care of. It's a long time ago, but I can remember her cooking to this day. Margaret stewed everything. I realised this pretty quickly as that was all I ever got. Chicken, beef, vegetables – it didn't matter what was prepared in the kitchen, it all came out stewed. And to follow it was rhubarb – always bloody rhubarb. With meals like that, it's no wonder I ended up supplementing my intake by living on doughnuts and sausage rolls – hardly the diet that today's sport nutritionists would recommend.

Another thing I couldn't stand about the digs was that the house had cats in it. I hate cats – they make me sneeze. I'm allergic to them – I can't breathe – so after tea at 5.30 or so I'd go straight to my room. One day I pulled the sheets back and there was a big dollop of cat's diarrhoea on it and, just to make matters worse, there were horrible white worms inside. Disgusting wasn't the word.

'Margaret!' I called out. 'Your cat's shat on my pillow!' and all she said was, 'Oh, my poor cat, he's ill.' Ill, my arse – not a word about my bed. I asked her if she was going to get rid of the cats and she said no, so I decided to take matters into my own hands. As soon as I could, I went down to the local joke store in Colchester and bought some itching powder – horrible stuff, the kind that stupid schoolboys sprinkle around. The next day I waited until I was alone in the house and got hold of the cats and poured loads of it on the back of their heads and shoulders. And then I waited.

Very soon, large bare patches appeared on their necks as their fur dropped out as the agonised creatures scratched and licked themselves in desperation. Margaret noticed, of course, and took them to the vet. I feared the worst and that my crime might be detected – this one might need some quick thinking to talk my way out of. But when Margaret came back with them, she said the vet had told her they must have picked something up when they were out. Result! I didn't say anything: I just put on my innocent, concerned look and left it at that. Well, they shouldn't have crapped on my pillow, should they? They never came into my room again. Job done.

A couple of times I would try to bring girls back to my digs but Margaret wouldn't let them in the house – it was like being tagged. I couldn't stand living there all the week, so on Wednesdays I'd get the bus home. It meant I could have a decent meal and also see a girl in Great Cornard called Julie Eagle. I was 16 and she was a bit younger. I never got hold of her, though it wasn't for want of trying.

Dad said if I was in the first team by 17 he would buy me a car. Boy, I would certainly deserve it if I did, given the type of games I was playing in. I was playing midfield for Colchester's reserves in the Town and County League, which, obviously, meant the games would be in and around the area. I think I played in three or four good footballing games – the rest were fights as we played around East Anglia at back-of-beyond places like Histon in Cambridge. Talk about inbreeding – sometimes it was like a scene from the film *Deliverance*. The local players had 12 toes and three ears – the good-looking ones, that is – and they wanted to eat you rather than play football against you.

Some of the grounds had floodlights that looked as though they were erected about the time electricity was discovered, and some didn't have floodlights at all. A good gate was around 100, although, when Colchester sent a side down, that might put an extra 30 or 40 on the attendance. Big time or what?

Now here's the funny thing – I loved it. I knew I had to play my best in every game if I wanted to get in the first team, and I was determined to do so. Even at those God-forsaken grounds with a cold Fenland wind coming off the North Sea whipping around your legs and a local missing link trying to cut you in half, it was still great. It was taking me where I wanted to go. I had to make sure that every game was my best if I wanted to get in the first team.

One game for the reserves was at Layer Road against Tiptree United – and they call it the Glory Game – when I was still just 16. At the time, Colchester had a fairly new signing in Roger Osbourne who, just three years earlier, had scored the only goal of the game when Ipswich beat Arsenal in their surprise 1978 Cup Final victory. Roger had scored the goal and then fainted – the heat and the emotion got to him – so he was promptly substituted. One thing was for sure: he was unlikely to collapse through high temperatures and excitement playing for Colchester reserves.

I was starting my career while he was, if not exactly finishing his, at least on the final leg, although he went on to give Colchester several more years' really good service. Roger was a Suffolk man and a smashing guy, and he and I were in the central midfield. A couple of times I thought he should have given me the ball so I said to him, 'Roger, next time!' It happened again and I shouted, 'Are you fucking blind? Give me the ball!' He could hear me – everyone could hear me, on and off the pitch. I didn't see anything wrong with it, and I still don't. Off the pitch, be as respectful as you like, but on the pitch we are all equal – it doesn't matter who you are or how many medals the other guy has got. All I was saying is that he should have given the ball to me. It didn't strike me as wrong that a 16-year-old should have a go at a man who recently wrote himself into football history in our neck of the woods.

We ended up drawing 1–1 but it seemed I'd done it again – I'd disgraced myself somehow. Afterwards, Ray Bunkell had a go at me and said, 'You should have shown him more respect.' But the one person who didn't mind was Roger himself. He knew what I was on about and why I had shouted at him. He knew I wanted to get on and that was just part of it as far as I was concerned. There was nothing personal in it and in no way was I doing him down. And he should have given me the bloody ball anyway.

I was playing well for the reserves and scoring some goals, so, just after Christmas, in January 1982 – still three months off my 17th birthday – I went to see manager Roberts. 'What are my chances, Boss?'

'Chances of what?'

'I think I'm better than those who are playing in the first team,' I said. 'I'm better than them all. I think my performances warrant it.'

'Oh, do you?'

I wasn't one to give in easily, so I asked if I hadn't had good reports on me.

He said he'd heard I was good on the ball but not too good defensively. 'Knuckle down and maybe your chance will come.'

Patience isn't a virtue most 16-year-olds have and I was no exception. So, when, soon after that, we had a reserves home game against Sudbury, my home-town team, I was revved up for it. The first team were watching before getting on board their coach for an away game and I knew that this was my chance to shine.

If I say so myself, for the first 20 minutes I was unbelievable. Everything I did came off. My old man was in the stands and gave me the thumbs-up, and for me that was like Pele saying I was playing well. We won 2–1 and the first team and manager saw enough before they left for me to reckon I'd impressed them. The headline in the local rag *The Suffolk Free Press* was GROVES SHOWS THE WAY and the opposition manager was quoted as saying, 'I wish we had a few like him.'

I even remember we picked up £6 for the win, so I reckoned I was knocking on the door, although I did manage one of the worst performances of my life soon after at Stowmarket. When I was shite, I was really shite, because I never hid. Talk about one step forward, two steps back.

Even so, there were a lot of injuries around the first-team squad and we had a home game one Tuesday night soon afterwards. The team sheet went up with 'sub to be announced' on it and I thought I was in with a chance. We were told to report to the ground by 5.30pm for the 7.30pm kick-off, but when I got there I discovered that another apprentice, Andy Gooding, was going to be the sub. I thought, What the fuck is going on? But I said good luck to him anyway, in the routine way footballers always do. I was 16 years and ten months and he was just over 17. He didn't get on anyway.

So on the Thursday it was in to see Bobby Roberts again. This time he set the ball rolling. In that charming way that Scotsmen have perfected over the years, especially when talking to Englishmen, he greeted me with a curt, 'Not fucking you again! What do you want?'

I said, 'Why wasn't I sub?'

Again, I got a cheery Caledonian response. 'What the fuck is it to do with you?'

Now I was scared of this gruff Scot, but I wasn't going to give in. There were some senior pros there who were frightened to knock on his door because of what they might hear – a few home truths – but I wasn't one of them. In for a penny, in for a pound. I stuck to my guns and, in fairness to Roberts, he then explained that Andy could cover for several positions and he didn't think I could.

After I went on for a while about how I deserved a chance and how good I was, he summed it all up by saying, 'That's in your opinion.' I guess by now he reckoned I was a pain for continually having a go at him, but I also think he liked the way this 16-year-old was determined to get in the first team. That's what he wanted.

Soon it was April 1982 and my 17th birthday was drawing near. I'd been training with the first team and one day I went to look at the reserve-team selection on the notice board at the ground and my name was missing. I was furious and really in the mood for a fight at being left out when I looked at the first-team list and my name was in there! I was in the squad of 17 for their game against Bournemouth.

I phoned my dad and told him and then Ray Bunkell told me to report to the Mill Hotel in town for the 11am pre-match meeting. I didn't think I'd play but I might be sub – that was the best I could hope for.

The next day, my dad took me to the hotel and when I walked in someone asked me, 'What do you want for your pre-match?' – meaning what would I like to eat. Mick Walker, our goalkeeper, always ordered scrambled egg on toast, so I just ordered the same. Even though I wasn't going to be playing, I was really nervous and couldn't think of anything else to say. Pretty stupid really, as I hate scrambled eggs and, when we sat down to eat, I just pushed it all away and ate the toast with my knife and fork.

Then Ray called us in for the team meeting and Bobby Roberts started going through the side. 'Number 1 Walker, number 2 Cooke...' As I said, I didn't think I'd be playing, so I wasn't really paying much attention, but then I thought I heard him say 'Groves...' I felt like nudging someone and saying, 'Did he just say me?' but I didn't have the nerve.

Then we got on to set-pieces and he said, 'Grovesy, you go to the edge of the box for this one...' So I had heard right – I *was* in the side! I was to become the first 16-year-old to play for Colchester's first team – and I couldn't tell anyone about it! This was in pre-mobile-phone days, remember. Still, I knew Dad would be at the game and all I could think about was that he'd promised me a car if I got in the first team by the time I was 17.

I got a lift to the ground but when we got there I didn't know what number I was meant to be wearing. I didn't know which peg to get changed under, so I waited for everyone else to get their shirts and there was the number 4 still hanging up. My boots were underneath it, so even I managed to work out that was for me.

As it was near the end of the season, it was a sunny day and there was a crowd of 2,662 to witness a momentous occasion in the history of football – my first-team debut. Colchester hadn't got much to play for but Bournemouth were pushing for promotion, so it wasn't going to be an end-of-the-season stroll in the park – not that that was my style anyway, and certainly not on my debut.

My nerves were unbelievable but I wasn't sick or had the runs or anything like that. The match kicked off and it was a lot quicker than I was used to, but I loved it. I loved the pace the game was being played at. I was grateful too for all those games I had played against bigger kids when I was a boy and how I had played against men when I was just 15. All the time I was thinking, This is great!

Bournemouth went 1–0 up and, although Ian Allinson equalised for the 'U's, they ended up beating us 2–1, but that didn't bother me too much. Of course, I would have preferred to end up on the winning team, but the main thing was I had made my first-team debut. I also remember I really smacked one shot that I thought was bound to end up in the net, but it hit the post and bounced clear. No player has a really bad debut, do they, so I was pretty pleased with mine and just annoyed that my shot hadn't gone in.

After the match, I went to clean up and, when I came out of the shower, there were all these boots lined up. 'Oi, superstar, these boots aren't going to clean themselves.' It was old Albert the kit man. There was more to come. The apprentices took it in turns to get the corner flags at the end of the matches and it was my turn. Just because I had played in the game made no difference. I had to get the flags and bring them back inside.

Afterwards, Dad gave me a lift back to Great Cornard and said, 'You did all right there, boy.' That was high praise indeed from him, so I said, 'Where is it then?'

'Where's what?' he said.

'The motor,' I said.

He laughed and said, 'Well, you've earned it.'

Bobby Roberts was quoted in the local paper as saying, 'Perry did well,' and another report, which managed to get my age wrong, said, 'One bright spot for Colchester was the impressive debut of 17-year-old Perry Groves. He worked manfully in midfield and his long throw was an asset.' Ah, that long throw – that was to come in useful in years to come.

The next morning I was up bright and early and down the local newsagents to see what the national newspapers had to say about me. The Sunday papers didn't carry reports on all the games, not the smaller ones anyway, but there was a Colchester–Bournemouth match report in the *News of the World*, so I bought a bundle of them and went home to read them. There was a line in the report that read, 'Colchester put the pressure on and hit the post through their young 16-year-old debutant Terry Grouse.'

Terry Grouse! Who the fuck was Terry Grouse?

Perry Groves had somehow become 'Terry Grouse' – my first mention in a national newspaper and they got my name wrong. Still, it was an early lesson that you can't believe everything you read in the papers and I knew it was me they were on about, wrong name or not, so I didn't care. And there would be lots more mentions – good and bad – in the future.

4

After my debut, I played all nine games left in that season, and every match I played I turned in a better performance than the one before. At least that was what I thought, and, although it might sound big-headed, it wasn't. When you are a player, no one knows better than you do how well or how badly you have done. So things were looking good for me.

Not so good for our manager Bobby Roberts, though – he got the sack. Cynics might say he obviously got the Order of the Boot for picking me, but that wasn't the case. His job had been in danger for a while and the local papers had been full of stories about how his days might be numbered after seven years in the job, lack of success, disagreement with the board – all the usual stuff.

Allan Hunter took over as player-manager – the same Allan Hunter I'd watched as a schoolboy when he was playing centre-half for Ipswich at Portman Road. He'd spent 11 years there and won more than 50 caps for Northern Ireland in the process, so there was no denying his playing record. He brought with him Cyril Lea, another old Ipswich hand, as coach. That's what happens in football: managers always want their own men around them.

I'd finished my first year as an apprentice and had another one to go, so the new Boss called me in. As always – and this was to be a constant factor throughout my career – my negotiating skills were fantastic.

'We are going to offer you a professional contract,' said Allan Hunter.

'Thanks,' I said.

Yes, I know – we aren't talking about the greatest businessman in the world here, are we? I was going to be on £55 a week at 17 and that would soar to £75 a week at 18. I actually though it was fantastic, to tell the truth.

It turned out, as it often does, that there was a hidden agenda. I'd played really well in the tail-end of the previous season when we'd beaten Crewe 3–1 away and Hunter and Lea had been in the crowd. Ray Harford, an old-fashioned centre-half who'd gone to Fulham as Malcolm Macdonald's coach, had also seen me play and liked what he saw, so I might be approached by them. Hunter and Lea knew they were going to be coming to Colchester and had obviously decided they didn't want me to slip out of their grasp.

Still, I was made up, but as always I came down to earth thanks to Dad: 'You can come home now and give your mum your keep.' So I did move back home – although I never gave Mum any keep. No one ever does, do they?

By now, you're probably wondering what had happened to Dad's promise to get me a car. So was I. But Dad was a man of his word, and I knew he wouldn't let me down. I was thinking in terms of a VW Golf or something fast and tricky like that, but what I got was a little different. Dad had a mate who ran a second-hand car place, so I ended up with a Vauxhall Viva that set him back about £150. The colour? Mainly rust actually, with a little bit of blue in between. Dad's thinking, and there was a certain logic to it, was why waste money on an expensive car when I'd probably have lots of accidents anyway?

My love life, however, was motoring along much more smoothly. I'd started going out with a local girl. It was with her that I first scored, so to speak. In her bedroom, if you must know, after we had in theory gone up to watch television. I didn't want to miss any of the programmes, mind, and if memory serves me right we managed it during one of the breaks for adverts. She had brown hair – although I'm in no position to talk about hairstyles – and she was a really nice girl who I won't name.

My mates, meanwhile, were fine about me signing for Colchester. None of them was jealous or anything stupid like that: it didn't bother them that I was a football 'star'. In the first place, Colchester were hardly Real Madrid, and I think they quite liked having a pal who was a professional footballer. Plus, they were real mates anyway.

During that summer, while I waited for the next season to start, I got a phone call from Tom the groundsman, my old buddy who had diabetic attacks, who never gave me a lift and whose cats shat on my pillow. He'd been left with just one apprentice to help him during the summer months, Andy Gooding. Tom wanted to know if I could help by coming in and helping seed the pitch as it was a lot for him and Andy to do by themselves.

Fair enough. He'd appealed to my better nature and I gave him the mature reply I thought was appropriate: 'You're having a laugh!' I explained to him that I was now a pro. I wasn't an apprentice any longer and so I didn't have to help seed the bloody pitch.

Old Tom muttered something about, 'I thought you might like to help your mate,' so I took that on board and decided to compromise. I went along and watched Andy do the seeding, and if I thought he was slacking I'd shout, 'You've missed a bit!' There's nothing like moral support, is there?

It ended up with me having nine weeks off that summer, but when we returned for pre-season training I was fighting fit: I'd been running every day and swimming a lot, I was teetotal – and all that shagging helped too.

With a new manager at the club, there's always a question mark about where you stand and whether you figure in his plans. Those early days are always fraught, but, if I say so myself, I helped matters by playing really well as the season started. I scored my first professional goal at home to Aldershot in the Milk Cup, a massive and unforgettable milestone in any player's career, but for once I'll let someone else do the talking. This is what one local paper had to say about the goal that helped clinch a 2–0 victory for us:

'Groves' goal came virtually out of the blue in the 35th minute. It was a beautiful volley from 25 yards out, a goal which the "U"s fans appreciated judging by the applause and cheers, and one that Groves himself will remember for a long time.'

Another reporter described it this way: 'A spectacularly curled shot from teenager Groves after 35 minutes provided the lead for the "U"s.'

Modesty dictates I should stop there, but what 17-year-old in the world would be modest about scoring their first goal in professional football? So here's one final report on that game, watched, incidentally, by a small but privileged crowd of 1,665 paying spectators: 'Groves planted the ball clean as a whistle to the top far corner of the net. The all-action kid from Cornard had another bright game and has adapted so quickly to league football.' I couldn't have put it better myself, actually.

We were either top or second in Division Four as the season got under way and things were looking good. Then stardom beckoned! OK, it wasn't Hollywood – it was Anglia TV, whose headquarters were in Norwich and were probably best known for a rather kitsch quiz show called *Sale of the Century* hosted by Nicholas Parsons.

As I've mentioned, in those days ITV's regional networks used to show highlights of the previous day's match from one of the teams on their patch on Sunday afternoons. I haven't any idea how many viewers tuned in that autumn Sunday in 1982 to watch *Match of the Week*, given that the match in question was Colchester against Blackpool. To be realistic, I can't imagine the pubs from King's Lynn to Coggleshall emptying as football fans downed their pints and raced home to watch it over their Sunday lunches. Hopefully, however, there were quite a few more than the 2,918 who actually paid to get in on the day.

But it was a big game for me. I was 17 and on TV playing professional football. Just to make my cup really runneth over, we won 4–1 and I scored. I can still remember it: I got the ball on the edge of the box, controlled it and rolled it into the corner.

That night's report of the match in the *Green 'Un*, the Saturday-night sports' paper, hit the nail on the head. 'Groves coolly rifled home a low shot,' it read. 'He had demanded the ball from Leslie square just outside the area and let fly into the corner out of the reach of the despairing Hesford.'

I've still got a video tape of that goal and, looking at it now, it's embarrassing really. I ran back to the centre circle and put my fist up towards my dad in the stands. It was a buzz, that's why – I knew it would be on TV and all my mates would be watching. To this day, I can remember being described as 'the red-haired number 4' on TV the next day.

Nowadays, a football star would probably fly his family to Dubai for a break to celebrate a good performance, or, at the very least, hire a restaurant for a blow-out with pals, girlfriend, family, etc. Me, I just went out with my girlfriend, probably to the Highbury Barn pub in Great Cornard – yes, that word 'Highbury' keeps cropping up – and downed a few lemonades with a shot of blackcurrant. I was still a non-drinker then and, although some of the lads at Colchester, those aged about 23 or 24, were into hard drinking, that wasn't my style. Not yet, anyway.

We were doing well in the Milk Cup and beat Aldershot, thanks, in part, to me smashing the ball into the corner of the net from 30 yards for one of the best goals I ever scored. That meant that we went in to the hat for the next round and were drawn to play Southampton home and away, a massive draw for Colchester. The Saints had Peter Shilton in goal and Alan Ball in midfield. Shilton was midway through a career that saw him win 125 England caps, still a record, and Ball will forever be remembered as part of the 1966 World Cup-winning side. I've got other memories of Mr Ball from much later in my career, but we will get to those in due course.

Playing a top side with internationals scattered through it was wonderful for Colchester. The Saturday before, we had a league match at Scunthorpe and drew 2–2, but I was only average. Not crap, not good, just average.

We were playing Southampton in the first leg in midweek and

we had a practice match the day before, first team against the reserves. Cyril Lea was handing out red bibs to the first team and the reserves were given yellow ones. I went to get a red bib and Cyril handed me a yellow one.

'I think you have made a faux pas there, young man,' I said.

'No, I haven't.'

'The first team are in red!'

'Yep, and you're in yellow.'

I was out. Bombed. Dropped. My world collapsed. I had taken it for granted that I would be playing and I had told everybody I would be. I was dazed: I couldn't believe it. I phoned my dad and I was crying my eyes out. Dad said I should talk to Allan Hunter. 'Go and see him,' he said. But by the time I got to Layer Road the ground was empty and Hunter had gone. Too late for explanations.

The following night it was a 13,000 sell-out crowd at Layer Road for the game and I thought I'd be substitute at least. Wrong again. The kick-off was at 7.30pm and I was in the stand in my sheepskin coat as the crowd were arriving. My pals spotted me and thought, Grovesy is a cool one – massive match ahead and him still in his suit just before kick-off! Then, still looking at me around 7.20pm, they realised I wasn't playing. Embarrassing or what?

The game kicked off – and I hoped Colchester would get hammered. Any professional footballer in the same position would have thought the same, and if they'd denied it then they'd be lying. I know that is how we think. Perhaps I am wrong – maybe I am the most selfish footballer ever to play the game – but I don't think so. As it was, it turned out to be a goalless draw and we lost in the second leg.

I'd also failed my driving test that week, so my world was really falling apart. Allan Hunter said nothing to me. I was out in the cold – in football terms, Siberia in December – and put in the reserves. It was an injustice, and crap man-management of a 17-year-old.

What had happened was that Cyril Lea wanted to play the long-ball game. I was frequently watching seagulls as the ball went up in the air and stayed there. The most serious injury I was likely to suffer was neck ache. I wasn't a 'dog' midfield player like, say, Robbie Savage is these days: a guy who just runs around snapping at the heels of everyone in midfield. So I was in the reserves, sometimes even the youth team. I thought I was giving it a go, but in all honesty my standards started to slip. Perhaps it didn't help that I was shagging my girlfriend before training, after training and in the evening.

It's an old cliché – like in the *Rocky* movies – that women can weaken your legs, but my dad was watching me play and he obviously thought I was seeing too much of her. On Friday nights, we would always have fish and chips at home, and one evening as Mum put the plate on the table in front of me she said, 'He's not very happy with you.'

Dad then came in and sat down and I said, 'What's the matter?'

He said, 'I don't know what you are doing with your life.'

Then came the bombshell. I was playing for the reserves at Soham Town Rangers the next day and Dad had watched virtually every game I had ever played in – school, the Dynamos, trials, Colchester. Now he said, 'I'm not going to watch you play tomorrow. You are wasting your career. With the talent you've got, you are wasting your life. I can't stand watching you do this.'

Then he started to cry. Now Dad is a hard man from the East End and I had never seen him cry before. I started to cry too.

'You are spending too much time with that girl,' he said. He didn't actually ask me to stop seeing her, but I got the message.

Mum just said, 'He's right.' Mind you, she always agreed with him. I think I was more devastated by that conversation than anything else in my career. It was heartbreaking.

The following day we turned up at Soham to find that the apprentice had forgotten to pack our boots – from personal experience, I know that's easily done – so four of us had to go down to the local sports shop and buy some new ones. Great. I played the first half and I didn't pull any trees up. Then I looked up and in the corner of the ground, practically hiding from view, were Mum and Dad. He'd obviously decided that morning that I needed his support, and he was right.

The rest of the season was a write-off really. I got three or four games as a sub. We played at Hartlepool and it was bleaker than Bleak House on a bleak Easter Monday. But at least I came on and scored as we beat them 4–1. The rest of the side decided to congratulate me by picking up handfuls of mud and throwing them all over me just to get my clean shirt dirty. They had one shower there and a bath that only took two guys at a time. As I was the youngest I had to wait until last to get clean. Yes, I ended up coming out dirtier than when I'd gone in.

That was one of the away trips that stays in my memory, alongside one of the first 'overnights' I ever had. Because of lack of cash, Colchester hardly ever stayed at hotels before an away match. It was usually a day trip, unless the ground was something like four hours or more away. We probably only had three or four overnights a season.

So when we had to play Blackpool it was a big deal and Mum packed my stuff for the trip in a sports bag and a suit-carrier. Just before the coach set off, I felt peckish, so I hopped off to get a snack, something healthy like a packet of crisps. I got back on as the last one to board the bus – and wished I hadn't, because my teammate Roy McDonough was sitting at the front of the coach wearing my pyjamas. He'd gone through my bag, the bastard, and found my jim-jams. They were the terribly old-fashioned type with stripes and a cord to tie around the waist, like something out of *Carry On Nurse*. Everyone was pissing themselves, and even the coach driver started pipping his horn.

One thing all footballers seem to have in common is that once they find something funny they don't let it go. Roy wore those pyjamas for the entire four-and-a-half-hour drive and even had them on as we walked into the hotel to check in. At least I got them back by bedtime.

One of the few other hotel stays that we had came over the New Year period. Back in pre-history, the lower divisions of professional football had been divided into the Third Division (North) and the Third Division (South). Colchester and Torquay United had both been in the southern section, and the legacy of this was that the annual holiday fixture saw us playing them on New Year's Day. What a local derby! It's only a round-trip of 600 miles between the two grounds, that's all.

We travelled down on New Year's Eve and, after we'd checked into our hotel, Allan Hunter said, 'Go to your rooms and come down at 11.15 and have a pint to see the New Year in.' So we met up in the snooker room late that evening and Roy McDonough said, 'Right, let's get the drinks in.' He started taking the order and most of the lads plumped for a lager and a few of them chose bitter.

I was desperately thinking what to order – shit, the pressure! I didn't want a pint like the rest of them, but I didn't want to seem a wimp. Roy had ordered something like 11 lagers and four pints of bitter and then he turned to me. All I could think of were drinks I'd seen knocked back at Christmas.

'I'll have a pint of Snowball, please', I said in my Joe Pasquale voice. In my head it had to be either that or a Babycham.

'Are you taking the piss?' said Roy.

I told him I wasn't and, as the rest of the lads started laughing, off he went to the bar to get the round in. When he came back with all the drinks on it, there was my pint of Snowball practically hidden under cherries, little umbrellas, straws, the lot. This was around the time the actor Oliver Reed was always in the newspapers for being drunk, so Roy handed me my pint of this thick yellow liquid, saying, 'Here you are, Ollie....'

It took me an eternity to finish it, and for months after that I was called 'The Snowball Kid'. It could have been worse, mind – I could have asked for a pint of Babycham!

As the year wore on, I did split with my girlfriend. Her dad called me in and said, 'Have you thought about your future?'

I said, 'No, I haven't'. It was swivel-chair time, folks. By that, I mean swivel it around and head for the door as quickly as possible – and keep running.

But there was a bird on the single-decker bus to Colchester in the mornings who I liked the look of anyway. Justine Brett had long blonde hair and I fancied her. I even followed her once after she got off the bus but I didn't have the courage to start chatting to her. After that, I didn't see her for a month until I realised she was getting the earlier bus to get to the Colchester Institute on time. So I got an earlier bus than I needed to and she was on it. I was clutching my boots and looking for somewhere to sit. She caught my eye and patted the empty seat alongside her and said, 'There's a seat here'. No mistaking that message. I was in there like a rat up a drainpipe and we went out for 14 months.

I had to use the bus as I'd failed my driving test for a second time. Most people take it in their stride, but not me. I wrote to the Driving Test Centre and said the same man had failed me twice and he had vendetta against me, so I wanted a different examiner for my next attempt! They sent me back a standard reply, but I did get a different guy for the third test and I passed it. It didn't make all that much difference to my lifestyle, however, as I was driving around on my own without 'L' plates anyway.

5

By the time the next season kicked off, Allan Hunter had resigned as manager, as he had been asked to let some players go and I don't think he could do it. Cyril Lea was in charge and he wanted 'runners' or 'dogs' or hammer throwers or whatever. He certainly didn't want me.

He called me in and said, 'It ain't working out, so we're prepared to let you go.'

Even though I had no agent and I was still only 17, I knew I had a contract, so I said to him, 'Give me a year's money and I'll go.'

'No, you can just go,' he said.

'I'm not going anywhere,' I said.

So he started playing me on the right wing for the reserves. I was really quick, but I thought he wanted to play me there, out of position, because he wanted me to go. There was a guy called David Hubbick who was ahead of me in Cyril Lea's opinion and he got chosen for the first team. He wasn't even full-time – he was a van driver by day, yet he was preferred ahead of me. I thought, Fuck you. In fact, that summed up my attitude.

One thing I will say about Cyril Lea, though, was that he was very much into fitness. He taught me how to look after my body, and I thought I started to play really well in the reserves. Eventually, I got back into the first team. But around this time Ian Allinson was transferred to Arsenal and he was popular with the crowd, so when I came back into the reckoning they weren't too keen on me. My pace was good and I was ripping full-backs apart but my crosses were useless and, to be honest, my finishing was pants too. I was playing well but there was no end product to show for it.

Still, we were drawn at home to Second Division Charlton Athletic in the FA Cup, another big game for the 'U's. Charlton had a guy playing for them called Ronnie Moore, who later went on to be a successful manager in the lower divisions. He'd done the rounds and, at one stage, when he was at Cardiff, the goals dried up to such an extent that some of their supporters made badges saying: 'I saw Ronnie Moore score.' Who said the Welsh weren't sarcastic?

Anyway, there was a bit of a kerfuffle involving him and Andy Farrell, our right-back. He said, 'Fuck off, son – how much have you got in the bank?' In other words, he was saying that we were on peanuts and he was worth a lot more. Andy obviously didn't get the put-down and with a quizzical look, said, '£37.83, but what's it got to do with you?' As verbal slanging matches go on a football field, that must have been one of the strangest. If only the fans knew what was going on!

I was on fire in that game, but at one point I took a bad touch and a Colchester fan standing on the terraces shouted, 'Groves, you ginger-haired wanker, you are shit!' This so-called fan was a big, fat, ugly slob who looked like Jabba the Hutt out of *Star Wars*.

I wasn't going to stand for that, so forgetting the game for a moment I turned to him and said, 'What did you say?'

Lo and behold, he repeated it. So I just said, 'The pies are over there – just leave some for someone else.'

We lost the match 1–0 and that should have been that, but it wasn't, because the fat bastard wrote to the club and complained. Cyril Lea called me in and said the chairman wanted to fine me. I said, 'What, because of that big, fat Jabba the Hutt bloke? He called me a useless ginger-haired twat. If you fine me, I'll go the PFA.' Now that would be an interesting test case if the Professional Footballers Association went into battle, because a player had been verballed and decided to answer fire with fire.

Talk about a problem! This was something Cyril hadn't come across in the coaching manuals. Then he said, 'What if I get him in, then you can apologise?'

I said, 'Yeah, get him in' – but I made sure I didn't say that I would apologise.

Anyway, the bloke eventually wobbled in. He had been easy to find as he was well known in the area. 'I have come for your apology,' he said.

'I didn't say I would apologise.'

He muttered something about it was disgraceful the way I had behaved in front of children – and he was the one who'd had a go at me!

So I told him, 'I'll take you to the Race Relations Board. You called me a fucking useless ginger twat.'

'No, I did not.'

'The thing I object to is "ginger",' I told him. 'That is racist. "Useless twat" would be fair enough. Would you like it if I came to your work and slagged you off?'

Then I told this man, who looked as though he earned a living as Pukka Pies' main taster, 'I'm prepared to forget it.' So we shook hands and that was that. But I never apologised. Poor Cyril had been standing there watching all this in disbelief – so much for the great public-relations exercise of having me say sorry to this knob! He just looked at me as Jabba waddled off and he shook his head.

As the season rumbled on, I was back in the first team. Having being told to get out at the start of the year, it ended with me being offered another 12-month contract for what would be my third year at Colchester. I was going to get £100 a week, and I went out and got a second-hand Ford Capri Ghia to celebrate. It was green with leather seats and cost me £700.

I started the next season on the right wing We had a much younger team and a lot of them were to move on to bigger clubs. Tony Adcock went on to Manchester City, goalkeeper Alec Chamberlain moved to Everton, Keith Day went to Orient, Andy Farrell to Burnley and Rudi Hedman was transferred to Crystal Palace. We were all aged around the 18, 19, 20 mark and we were very fit. Often, after training, we would come back in the afternoon without any coaches around. My pace was getting me into great positions, but my crossing and finishing needed to improve.

As we had a lot of young players in the starting-line up by then, when we played at home on a Friday night we'd invariably attract a large number of scouts from the bigger clubs. There were several reasons for this. First, there were no other games to watch on a Friday evening. Second, it was good for their expenses to travel all the way to Colchester; and, third, it got them away from their wives on a Friday night. What more could a man want?

Tony Adcock was scoring loads of goals for us and we were

dangerous as a striking force, although we weren't so good away from home. But I scored 12 goals that year and I was playing the way I wanted to. Stewart Houston had arrived at the club as player-coach – a big name for us: a Scottish international who'd played for Manchester United – and I was learning all the time. Colchester was a stepping stone for me, but I just loved playing football – period.

Then I picked up an injury and when I came back I was sub for a home match. There was only one sub allowed in those days, and goalkeeper Alec Chamberlain was our 13th man, so to speak. Our physiotherapist Charlie Simpson had also picked up an injury, so, although he was on the bench in case anyone got a knock, he wasn't able to run on to the pitch. That meant that, if anyone needed the magic-sponge treatment, Alec would have to provide it. Alec, who's from Ramsey in Cambridgeshire, kept asking what he'd have to do if someone got injured, so I said, 'Don't worry, I'll help you.' Fool that he was, he believed me.

Alongside the bench was a big bucket filled with cold water. Inside that was a douche bag and the sponge itself was inside the bag. To tell the truth, that bucket was so big, it was more like a barrel. Anyone with their wits about them would realise that, if someone got a knock, you should scoop the douche bag out of the water, go on the pitch with that, and when you got to the injured player take the sponge out and slap it on.

But not Alec. And I wasn't going to enlighten him. 'Big fella,' I said to him, 'if someone gets hurt, you take the bucket on with you.' He fell for it. Soon one of our guys got hurt and I turned round to the crowd behind me, pointing at the bucket and mouthing, 'Just watch this.'

The rain was pouring down and Alec was only wearing trainers, so this sortie was doomed from the start. Have you ever tried to run with a bucket full of water? It's impossible. It's difficult enough to run with a bucket when it's empty, let alone when it has a few gallons in it. Too late Alec realised he'd been had. He was out there in the middle of the pitch, too far to turn back, not far enough to complete his mission. The inevitable happened and he and the bucket went flying on the greasy surface like something out of Fred Karno's Circus. When he came back, he really slaughtered me. It didn't harm his career, though, as Alec went on to earn his living in league football for over 20 years at Everton, Luton, Sunderland and Watford.

At Christmas 1984, I split up with Justine. Her dad probably saw me as an urchin not going anywhere – wonder where he could have got that idea from? – so that put the kybosh on that. He was a window-cleaner and I saw him up his ladder in Sudbury soon after. I started booting his ladder but he wouldn't come down.

If Ipswich had a home game on a Tuesday night, I used to go and watch them and I'd think, I can do that. I wasn't overawed by the standard of their play. Also, a few of their older players came to us at the end of their careers and I knew I could hold my own with them. I kept saying to myself that, if I did not get away by the time I was 21, I would be destined to play in the lower divisions all my life.

That season, we got drawn against Swansea City, then managed by John Toshack, in a two-leg Cup match and drew 0–0 at their place. I ripped them apart but missed a series of one-on-ones against their goalkeeper, Jimmy Rimmer. I couldn't have hit a cow's arse with a banjo that night, or most nights come to think of it.

In the second leg at our place, Tony Adcock scored with a fantastic chipped goal. Emlyn Hughes had moved to Swansea by this time and was playing at the back for them, and after the match he walked towards me, getting ready to shake hands. 'You are different class,' he said. 'You're too good for this place.'

Just as I was about to come out with some modest response, old Crazy Horse kept on walking straight past me and shook Tony Adcock's hand. It was Tony he was talking to all the time. It meant a lot to Tony, I can tell you. It meant a lot to me too, and he wasn't even talking to me!

In the season 1985–86, I carried on scoring and even got two hat-tricks. One of them was at Southend in a top-of-the-table game when I was being marked by the former West Ham full-back Frank Lampard. Frank is the father of the current Chelsea and England star, whom he decided, with great originality, also to call Frank. I'm happy to report that I gave Frank Senior a real roasting in our 4–2 victory and left him trailing behind me time after time. I even made the fourth goal, just to round it off. Towards the end of the game when I got the ball, rather than tackle me he would turn away from me and start running back towards his own goal, just so that he had a head start when I set off. It didn't do him much good though.

I got the match ball afterwards and Frank came into the players' lounge with a bottle of champagne under each arm. I reckoned at least one of them must be for me.

'All right, son?' he said.

'What's the champers for?' I asked, to which he replied, 'My man-of-the-match award.'

Roy McDonough said sarcastically, 'I'd hate to see what he gets when he plays well.'

I scored another hat-trick against Southend when I was playing centre-forward in an LDV Trophy match and Tony Adcock was also playing well: by Christmas he'd got something like 28 goals in all competitions. Just before Christmas, without my asking for it, my pay went up to £150 a week and my contract was extended by 18 months, and the club said I was one of their best-paid players. Yeah, good call.

I got sent off for the first time too. We were at Darlington and there was a bit of a skirmish near the touchline when the ball went out for a throw-in to us. At least, it should have been, but the linesman gave it to Darlington. I called him a twat and then he flagged. The referee came over and said, 'You're off,' so off I went – and after just 20 minutes too. We ended up losing 4–0 and on the way back home – and it's a long journey from Darlington to Colchester – a couple of the players said I'd let them down.

When the referee's report came in, it said I had called him 'a fucking useless twat'. I appealed against the sending-off, saying I had only called him a 'twat', but it didn't do any good. I lost the appeal and I was banned for two games.

Although I was playing well, our form as a team faded a bit after Christmas and Cyril Lea got the sack around March. Our old goalkeeper Mick Walker, who had been my roommate on some of my early away trips, took over on a temporary basis. Many footballers have nicknames, but Mick had one of the poorest nicknames ever. He was called 'Bures' during his playing days because he came from Bures, a village in Suffolk. Original or what? It's a good job he wasn't from Bury St Edmunds.

So Mick, who had been the reserve-team coach, now became caretaker manager and a man called Jonathan Crisp became chairman. He didn't rate me and reckoned I wasn't going anywhere. I had a different opinion, so I put in a transfer request and made it clear I reckoned I was too good for Colchester and wanted to take my game to a higher level. The answer came back no, but Bures – sorry, Mick Walker – called me in and handled the situation very well. He said, 'Play to get away and I'll keep you informed.'

Now I should mention for the first time a man who became very important in my life: John Hazell, a financial adviser based in Colchester. I had gone to him when I got my first contract so he could give me some advice about setting up a pension, getting a mortgage, all that sort of stuff. John's clients included Bobby Robson, the former England manager, and George Graham. John was never my agent but he would advise me on my contracts and investing my money.

It was John who contacted me one day to say that Crystal Palace were interested in me. It was the first I'd heard about it but Palace, who were then in the Second Division, had offered £40,000. A little while later, Ian Evans, who was assistant coach at Palace, telephoned and asked if I would like to sign for them. They'd been watching some bloke in non-league football and thought I'd be good to play up front with him. The other fella's name, by the way, was Ian Wright!

I thought, Great – this is just the gee-up my career needs. I was wondering who had been watching me in training – were there spies up in the trees? But nothing happened – it all just faded away.

By this time, my hairstyle had become a mullet, popular in the 1980s with the likes of Mel Gibson, Ian Botham and Chris Waddle. That meant it was curly on top, short at the sides, but long down the back. On top of that, my nickname – and I've had a few over the years – was 'Perse' after Percy Sugden, the resident know-all on *Coronation Street*. I guess the other lads thought I was a know-all too.

Anyway, at the end of the season we were playing Hartlepool

at home and were 0–1 down with just ten minutes left when I went past their full-back – only for him to yank my hair at the back. It hurt like hell and I must admit I lost it. Their goalkeeper threw the ball to the full-back and I went steaming in. I gave him a superb Cantona – a two-footed high tackle – with one foot catching him in the ribs and another in the waist. He disappeared off the pitch, over the wall and into the crowd, and I could hear him groaning. I just walked towards the dressing room. There was no point in waiting to be sent off – I knew I would be going.

When I got to the dressing room, I just sat there thinking, What am I doing with my life? Then I heard some cheers, and then some more cheers. A few moments later, the game ended, the door burst open and the lads streamed in. 'Top man, Perse!' shouted one player. 'Well done, Percy!' said another. We'd only gone and scored twice in the last ten minutes when I was off the field. Manager Mick Walker came in and said, 'Grovesy – superb. It changed the game. Well done. But you're fined two weeks' wages!'

That suspension meant I missed the first few games of the next season and it wasn't until our third match that I had a game, at home to Exeter. We drew 1–1 and I had a shocker. I had the rest of the weekend off, during which time I got a telephone call from John Hazell. 'Perry,' he said, 'you are not supposed to know this, but I know George Graham has been in for you and has asked for permission to speak to you.'

It didn't sink in for a moment, because George had been manager at Millwall for a while and I'd forgotten he'd recently replaced Don Howe at Arsenal. Then the penny dropped. 'You are joking, aren't you?' I said. I was speechless. I just hoped that Colchester weren't going to mess it all up by asking stupid money for me.

That night, Mick Walker rang me and said that the club had had an offer for me from Arsenal and they had accepted it. I simply said, 'Great, fine.'

Mick said, 'You don't sound very surprised,' and I replied, 'Just out of curiosity, how much?' Mick said that was a matter between the clubs.

Excitedly I phoned my dad and asked him to guess who'd come in for me. 'Crystal Palace?' he guessed. 'Ipswich? Norwich?' In the end, I put him out of his misery and told him it was Arsenal. All he said was, 'How good is that!' He didn't say anything else – he'd already summed it up perfectly.

Colchester told me to keep it quiet, so I said, 'Of course' – and then phoned everyone I knew straight away. I was like the town crier. I even telephoned the local newspaper but their sports desk was engaged.

The next day I was on the train to London with John Hazell, heading for Highbury and the start of my life with Arsenal. No one, least of all me, could guess what lay ahead.

6

As the train headed towards Liverpool Street station, I sat there in my suit and tie – even my shoes had been freshly polished – and told John Hazell exactly what my position was. 'I'm not in a strong negotiating position, am I? I'm on £150 a week and if I can get £250 or £300 I'll be happy. If I don't take this opportunity now, it may never come again.'

We took a taxi to the ground and as I stepped out I could almost smell the sense of history in the air. The ground had been Arsenal's home since 1913 and its wonderful East Stand – a Grade II-listed art deco building – had been built as Hitler was warming up for World War II. I had been to Highbury a couple of times to see my old pal Ian Allinson play, so I wasn't frightened or apprehensive. I knew this was where I wanted to be.

I walked up the stairs and into the famous marble entrance hall. On the floor of the hall, set in granite, was a motif of the club's cannon crest. From the hall, you could easily reach the tunnel leading to the pitch, the players' dressing room and the club box office. A bronze bust of Herbert Chapman, the legendary Gunners' manager who died in 1934, looked down on all visitors.

George Graham came down to meet us, immaculate in club blazer and tie. We went upstairs to his office with its elegant wooden panelling, and he sat behind his mahogany desk. His chair was massive, like a throne, while we had two little chairs to sit on. Great psychology!

George said he'd been watching me and wanted me to join the club, adding that he'd been following my career for a while, could tell I had the desire he wanted and had even tried to get me for £15,000 when he was at Millwall. That was the first I'd heard about that. He also added that the clubs had agreed a fee of £75,000 for me.

I had to say something, so I asked where I would play. The Boss, as he was soon to be, said he was buying me as a winger. 'Can you play on both sides?' he asked.

'Yes,' I insisted promptly, although I had never played on the left in my life.

George then said he expected me to spend my first season in the reserves, adding, as if he needed to, 'It's a big step up for you.'

I couldn't really say, 'Fuck that – I want to play first-team football!', could I?

My wages would be £350 a week and I'd get a signing-on fee of £5,000. I'd also get £150 appearance money – I had never heard of appearance money until then – and there would also be a £350 bonus for a win. On top of all that, I'd be getting a £2,500 disturbance allowance, to go towards my moving costs. It was to be a three-year contract and, if I did well, it would be reviewed during the course of it. I thought, What's the point in going away to think about it? I wasn't going to say no, was I? So I signed there and then. I had nothing to lose by signing, and I had no fear.

The Boss, as he most definitely was now, shook my hand and said, 'Congratulations.' Then he looked me in the eye and said, 'Now you are playing for the Arsenal I will tell you one thing: remember who you are, what you are and who you represent.'

Note that he said 'the Arsenal', not just 'Arsenal'. That's the way he always referred to the club, always putting the definite article in front of the club name. The dictionary says it's OK to do that if you are referring to something that is unique. That's how the Boss regarded the club, and so did I.

I was immediately taken for a medical and I remember thinking, What if they find a hole in the heart or something? but they didn't.

And in case anyone is wondering if there was a bung anywhere along the line, then no, there wasn't. The Boss was to eventually leave the club after a scandal over a payment he received, and he was banned from football for a year. But, hand on heart, I never saw any of that, let alone took part in it. I didn't even pay John Hazell who came with me – it was just understood that when I came to invest my new earnings then he would be the financial adviser I used.

I remember all this happened on 4 September, a Thursday, but the day went past in a blur. I headed for the nearest phone to give Dad the good news. He and Mum had split up by then and Dad was now running a pub in Ipswich. 'I'm over the moon for you, boy,' he said. 'Now the hard work starts, and you've got to prove to everyone that you are as good as I know you are.' I think Dad realised that his job was done – it was now up to me and the people at Arsenal.

We got back on the train at Liverpool Street and, as we headed back to East Anglia, I had this glowing feeling. Instead of saying to people, 'I am Perry Groves of Colchester', I would now be saying, 'I am Perry Groves of Arsenal'. Only one point – I thought I was worth more than £75,000.

Colchester, incidentally, and their new chairman Jonathan Crisp didn't do a very good deal with my transfer. They might have thought the amount paid for me was OK, but they failed to put a sell-on clause in the contract, which would have meant that when I moved to Southampton for £750,000 some years later they could have picked up 20 per cent – £150,000 – on the deal. That would have been a massive amount to a little club like Colchester, so whoever was in charge of the business side of the deal could have done better.

I was feeling generous, so I went to get two teas, telling John Hazell, 'These are on me'. Clutching the teas on the way back, I met Reg Nelson, a Colchester businessman who used to throw an end-of-season party for the players there. 'What are you up to then?' he asked, so I told him I'd just signed for Arsenal.

'Fuck off', he replied. 'Where have you been really?' But when I insisted it was true, he said, 'I'm really chuffed for you', and tried to buy me champagne. I told him I'd have a beer when I next saw him.

George Graham wanted me in for training the next day, a Friday, so as soon as the train pulled into Colchester station I went straight to Layer Road to pick up my boots. There was no one around, so there was no big emotional farewells or anything like that. I just put my boots in a bin bag and left. Simple as that. Incidentally, my mullet hairstyle was also in the past by this stage. I'd shaved it at the sides, so my Tintin look – the one I was to have for the next few years – was already well in place.

By now, I was dating Mandy Farrell, my wife-to-be, and I stayed at her parents' house that night and was up at 5am next day to get to Highbury on time. I took the tube from Liverpool Street to Highbury and was met by Steve Burtenshaw, who'd been caretaker manager before George arrived. We got into his BMW and, as we drove off to the club's London Colney training ground, he said, 'This is where the hard work starts.'

I had butterflies in my stomach as we sat in the car and all these famous players began arriving: England internationals Kenny Sansom and Viv Anderson, the crowd's favourite Charlie Nicholas, all arrived in their gleaming new cars. As they walked past, I was introduced to them all, and then to the backroom staff. There was Theo Foley the assistant manager, Gary Lewin our physio, Tony Donnelly the kit man with his broad Irish accent, Terry Burton the reserves manager and Pat Rice, a member of the famous 1971 Double side and by then youth-team manager.

What a difference from Colchester! There was a main pitch and about eight other full-sized pitches, all looked after by two full-time groundsmen. The changing rooms were in a modern building with loads of separate changing rooms, each easily capable of fitting in six or seven players, on either side of the corridor. Every changing room had its own showers and there were five or six individual baths. It was luxurious compared to Colchester, where we had had one bath between the lot of us. Different changing rooms were used by different players: the apprentices had some, then the reserve side had others and then the first-team squad of about 20 players had three rooms of their own near the end of the building.

Tony Donnelly's accent was so thick that I couldn't understand what he was saying to me most of the time. He also had the habit of ending every sentence with the word 'bump'. He'd say something like, 'Give me your boots, bump' or 'Here's your kit, bump'. Strange or what? Anyway, he told me my squad number was 15 and then he gave me a red sweat-top with 15 on the front. I didn't realise the significance of the colour straight away, but I discovered the young players had a blue top and there were about 20 to 25 red tops for the first-team players.

As we ran out on to the pitch, the Boss called out, 'Grovesy, you're with us – we are doing some set-pieces.'

I thought, I had better watch myself here – first impressions count. But it was all very easy – my corners were OK, even though I was nervous. I noticed that everything was done at a quicker tempo, but I liked that. Just about the only other thing I can remember from that first session was that there was a bunch of the younger players like David Rocastle and Stewart Robson, and that every time David Rocastle took a corner I'd shout out, 'Great ball, Rocky.'

Stewart Robson was the England Under-21 captain at the time. He lived out Brentwood way and after training he asked me where I came from. I told him Colchester and that I'd be getting the bus back to Highbury to make my way home. Stewart offered to give me a lift to Shenfield station, where I could easily pick up a train. After about ten minutes or so in the car, he said, 'Are you on a good deal then? I reckon he's put you on the same deal as us.' Then he asked me directly, 'How much did you get?' Presumably that was the real reason he had offered me a lift – he wanted to know my salary! I didn't tell him – and that was the only time he ever gave me a lift.

I never told anyone about how much I earned, and I never asked anyone either. As long as I thought I was on a fair deal, that's all that I cared about. If I was on £350 and some first-team players were on twice that, it didn't bother me. Other players, though, get eaten up by it, wanting to know what their mates earn and are envious if they find out it's more than they're on.

I couldn't get to the training ground by public transport, so obviously I needed a decent car. Unfortunately, I blew up three cars in my first week at the club.

First, I had an old MGB GT and the good news for me was that, as the Chelmsford by-pass had just opened, the journey of one and a half hours was reduced to one hour, as long as I had a car capable of getting there in one piece. The bad news was that, as I arrived at the car park at London Colney, it was like a scene out of *Chitty Chitty Bang Bang*. The head gasket had blown and steam was pouring out of the car. I had to take bottles of water back with me in the car and keep topping it up just to get home.

I told my dad about it that night and a bloke who was always at his pub lent me a Ford Granada like something out of *The Sweeney*. But the bonnet on it was busted and held down with string. There wasn't much future in keeping that car if the bonnet blew open every time the car reached 60mph.

Next came a Mini that Mandy's brother lent me, but that blew up too. All that first week I kept turning up in these different cars – the rest of the side must have thought I was some sort of second-hand car dealer. When my money finally came through, I bought myself a new Ford Escort. I could have got something flashy like some of the other players, but I reckoned that they had earned theirs, but I hadn't earned the right to have one just yet.

7

My first game for Arsenal was for the reserves at home to Oxford United at Highbury and – it goes without saying – it was a massive thrill for me. I stayed with my old Colchester teammate Ian Allinson on the Tuesday night to get ready for the game on Wednesday afternoon. It was just a normal game for Ian, but I was more nervous than I'd ever been before. We had Tommy Caton at centre-half and Graham Rix, an England international, was coming back from injury and he was in the side too. It was a big game for me, but I just loved the fact I was playing at Highbury and I didn't care that there was hardly anyone there. George Graham was there and so, of course, was my dad.

I was quite surprised at the pace of the game, but I did all right. We won 2-0 and I made one goal with my trademark long throw. I asked the Boss if I was getting Thursday off but he said, 'No chance – and you're in on Thursday afternoon too.' What he wanted was for me to get in synch with the way the team played. He wanted me to learn how to 'show people inside'. That was the Arsenal system he wanted to instil in all of us, where the opposition weren't allowed to get wide – we would make them go sideways, force them into congested areas of the pitch.

There was no reserve game that weekend, but the next week we were at Crystal Palace. We beat them 5–2 and I scored with a towering far-post header, although the full-back was only about as big as Ronnie Corbett. So I was pleased – I'd played half-decently and I thought I was settling in well.

At one stage during that game, a young lad was brought on. I thought he was 15 or 16, but it turned out he was a couple of years older than that. He was just a thin, blond stick of a lad but you could tell that he was a good player on the verge of breaking into the reserves. I always struggled to remember names when I went to a new club, and I thought this lad was called Mercer. In fact, it was Paul Merson, who was to become my massive mate at the club, have some great times with me and figure very largely in a lot of the trouble I was to get into.

Within three weeks, I'd got into the first-team squad and was training with them, so I was doing all right. We had a midweek Littlewoods Cup game with Doncaster Rovers, and my name was on the list of the 14 or 15 players for the game. We were winning 2–0 with about ten minutes left when the Boss said, 'On you go. Go up front and try to get a couple of early touches.' He didn't have to tell me twice.

I raced on and started running around like a Tasmanian Devil. I must have looked like a headless chicken out there. I remember I managed to flick one ball through to Charlie Nicholas, but the keeper saved his shot.

Next was a league game at Luton Town and again I was in the

squad. In those days, Luton had an artificial pitch and, although we would train on our own artificial surface and have a run-out on theirs, it was no good – you just wanted to get the game out of the way. But again I came on for the last ten minutes, and this time I was given my first greeting to the big time.

Luton had a giant centre-half called Steve Foster who'd made his name with Brighton and even picked up three England caps. He was a big man with a big barnet, usually kept in check by a white headband, and he decided to say hello to me in a defender's type of way. The ball was miles away as I ran past him and he tripped me up and sent me flying. The artificial turf ripped the skin off both my knees as I slid across it – it was agony. Fozzie, as he was known, just looked at me and said, 'You're playing with the big boys now, son.' Thanks a lot.

But all I cared about was that after the game, which we drew, I got an extra £175 for the draw and my £150 appearance money.

Things were on the move on the home front too. I had told Mandy we would not get married until I was earning good money. 'If I get a decent move, we'll get married,' I'd promised her. I thought I'd given myself a year, but George Graham came along and messed all that up! But I was now able to buy a house on my Arsenal wages, so I decided to move from Ipswich, where I had been staying, to Colchester. I bought a three-bedroom house in the High Woods part of town for £40,000.

Remember that £2,500 disturbance allowance I'd been given when I signed for the Gunners? Well, obviously, my little move didn't come to anything like that, but I got a receipt from one of my mates for £2,400 and claimed that back from the club, so I made a profit on the transaction.

Mandy was old-fashioned in the sense that she wouldn't move in with me until we were married, which was fair enough. More to the point, it meant that I was Billy Bachelor, living alone in a house with three beds. I was still only 21 and none of my mates had their own places yet, so all the action took place 'Chez Pez'. It was surprising how attractive I had become to the ladies: I was suddenly much better looking now I'd signed for Arsenal.

Occasionally, though, I'd get some blokes who would come up to me in pubs near by and say, 'Aren't you that prat who played for Colchester?'

My reply to that was, 'Sorry, I don't know your name,' and they would reply 'Well, we know yours.' So then I'd say, 'Exactly.' I never back down from guys like that. I know you are meant to walk away, but I never did.

The big news, though, was that I was about to make my full debut. Graham Rix was injured and the Boss called me in on the Thursday and asked, 'Can you play left side?' Well, half the time I didn't use my left foot at all, but I told him that of course I could.

We were playing at Nottingham Forest, one of the few clubs where the manager was more famous than the players. That was because it was Old Big 'Ead himself, Brian Clough. What a day to remember, and behind me was the most capped left-back in England's history, Kenny Sansom. I was used to full-backs saying, 'Come back and help me out.' There was none of that with Kenny. It was a piece of piss – once the game had started, he talked me through it and kept saying, 'Go away, leave him to me.' He didn't need any help. Oh, and Ian Allinson also came on as sub, so there were two Colchester boys on the field for the Arsenal.

Forest were near the top of the table at this early stage of the season and, although we lost 2–1, I thought I'd played well. As I've said before, I'd rather I played well and lost than the other way round. And I got another £150 appearance money – I couldn't get over that.

I saw my dad briefly in the bar after the game, and then we got on the coach to come home. I couldn't believe what I saw. All the tables on the bus had been laid out with placemats and cutlery, and there were two lads in black trousers and white coats ready to serve a meal. I was used to fish and chips after a game, but here we could have salmon or melon to start, followed by chicken or fish or pasta as a main course. After that, it was crumble and custard, and a cheeseboard or fruit. At one stage, I got up to get myself a drink and one of the waiters told me, 'No, don't do that. We'll get it for you.' There was no alcohol but I couldn't believe the meal and the way it was served, compared with the lifestyle I'd been used to at Colchester.

The Boss would sit at the front of the coach with Theo and Gary Lewin, and if you had a knock or a swelling you had to go and see them and they would give you anti-inflammatory tablets, two to be taken that day, two tomorrow. The problem was that you couldn't drink if you were taking them, so lots of the players just threw the things away. Some of the pills were so strong that they gave you the shits too.

There was – and still is – an etiquette to be observed that, if you've lost a match, you can't be seen to be happy and enjoying life on a return journey. But I was sitting there feeling really contented because I knew I wasn't out of my depth playing football at this level.

It was in these early days that I noticed George Graham's attention to detail. It was fantastic. He was the first to have a detailed report prepared on all the opposition players, and there would be three or four A4 pages on every team with remarks like 'ball-watcher', 'likes to overlap' or 'give him a dig early on'.

George obviously wanted to bring the younger players, like me, into the reckoning. He wanted guys he could ingrain his methods into, including pushing the opposition inside – not like the way Kenny Sansom and Viv Anderson normally played at full-back where the opposition could go down the line. I think the Boss was working on ideas he had got from his days as a player at the club and from his mate Terry Venables. You didn't have to be a genius exactly, but you did need a brain to make the system work.

In truth, George needed to do something, because the club had had a bad five years and was in the doldrums. They certainly had individuals who could play a bit, but the club was underachieving and home crowds were down to 22,000–25,000 at times. George was determined to change all that. An example of that was that, within a week of arriving at the club, a tailor had come to the ground and taken my measurements. Soon I had a smart blue Aquascutum blazer with our gun badge on it, a red silk tie and immaculate grey slacks. You had to wear the outfit, with tie, on all public appearances. George felt it sent out the message 'We are the Arsenal' to everyone and I think he was right.

So the stage was sent for my home debut. On the Thursday, the Boss said to me, 'How do you feel about playing up front?' Back came the usual answer: 'All right.' The away fans had seen me but the home fans hadn't, so this was the debut that counted. I was determined to do well against a Watford side that had Tony Coton in goal, Kenny Jackett, Luther Blissett and a slim John Barnes, before he got big, on the wing.

There were only 24,076 inside Highbury on 11 October 1986 to witness this historic moment – not a big crowd at all, but the largest I had ever played in front of. And after only 20 minutes I scored.

I remember all the goals I scored – yes, I know that wouldn't be too hard – but this one sticks in the memory for obvious reasons. I collected the ball from a throw-in and wanted to control it on my thigh. But I miscalculated and it rolled away from me towards the 18-yard line. I thought, I'm going to have to bend this, and that's exactly what I did – and with my left foot too. Tony Coton was left waving to the stands as he tried to stop it and it thumped against the stanchion.

Watford equalised through Mark Falco soon after the restart, but in the 58th minute Steve Williams put me through for a one-on-one with Coton. I took a touch, but it was the touch of a rhino and the ball went too far. Coton came out and I knew I was not going to score. Now it so happens I was always good at tipping it round the keeper and then falling over him, so I touched it away and he brought me down. It was definitely not diving, by the way – just playing in a way that meant that, if the keeper didn't make sure he avoided me, he'd end up giving away a penalty. His stupid fault really.

It was the same with full-backs. Tackling from behind was allowed in those days, and I reckoned that once I got in the area it was payback time. If I thought I was going to score then I'd stay on my feet, but if I thought the chance wasn't there and a tackle came in... thank you very much, referee.

Coton and I both knew that I could have avoided him, but I stayed down and made sure I avoided eye contact with him. Like all good goalkeepers, he was a nutcase, after all, and you don't poke a bear in the eye with a sharp stick. Coton didn't like it and, after heated words with the referee and linesman, he was sent off. Their midfield player Nigel Callaghan went in goal and almost saved Martin Hayes's penalty. Near the end, Niall Quinn got another for us, so we ended up winning 3–1.

In all honesty, that was the best game I ever played. I should have retired there and then! The fans just loved me. I was new and raw, and most of them were thinking, Who is this kid? Perhaps I gave them too many expectations. Still, they had a few nicknames to think about: 'Tintin', 'Neil Kinnock', 'Shirley' (as in Temple) were all in the frame.

The Boss gave us the usual debrief afterwards and, when you won, he played down the faults and stressed the good points. He told me I had made some good runs but I needed to work on my hold-up play.

To make my home debut was wonderful, but to score was even better and it took that pressure off me. I couldn't resist it: I bought all the papers the next day to see my name in them.

I was in the papers again soon afterwards when we played at Southampton. Tim Flowers, who was really just starting his career, was in goal for them in place of the injured Peter Shilton, and again Steve Williams put me through in a one-on-one with the keeper. He thought he was going to get it, but I knew he wasn't. My right boot caught him in the face and I thought I'd broken my foot as the impact was so hard, so it must really have hurt him.

I looked round and there he was lying on the floor and all his cheek was smashed in. Everyone came out to look at him, including our physio, and one of their outfield players had to go in goal. Just to add insult to his injury, the ref awarded us a penalty! Colin Clarke went in goal, we scored and after that we ran out 4–0 winners, and I even got the last goal to round off a good day at the office.

Good for me that is – poor old Tim ended up with a fractured cheekbone, an operation in hospital to repair it and having to drink through a straw for a while. Afterwards, I wondered what I should do to say sorry to him. I decided to send him some flowers in hospital. But then I thought, Blokes don't do that, do they? and I didn't want anyone thinking I was a poofter or anything like that. But I sent them to him anyway, and I'm glad I did as when I eventually ended up at Southampton he was there, and when I walked in the dressing room he said, 'I think you owe me an apology.'

I said, 'Shut up or I'll break the other cheekbone.' We were both laughing though – honest.

I had got in the Arsenal side because of a knee injury to Charlie Nicholas that kept him out for four to six weeks. The side went on a 22-match unbeaten run, and I knew that George wouldn't change a winning side, so even when he was fit Charlie couldn't get back in the team. We were top of the league and everything looked rosy. The fans must have thought George's judgement of his players was great and I was enjoying playing with better players than I had been used to.

Now I've got quite a few stories about what we got up to in years to come when we hit the town, but I don't think Arsenal was a drinking club by any means at that stage. Some of the players would go to Stringfellows, sure, but I wasn't part of that clique. I would just go home to Colchester and if I wanted a drink I would go out with my mates.

But things changed when we went on an Arsenal 'bonding' trip to Albufeira in Portugal. English teams were banned from European competitions at this time, so the fixture list wasn't as congested for the top clubs as it is now and we were able to go away for some fun in the sun.

Bonding – that's one word for it. You should know that at this stage that, while Charlie Nicholas and I didn't *not* get on, we weren't the best of friends either. He would take the piss out of me and I would take it back out of him. Charlie decided he was social secretary for the trip – the one who organises play time, so to speak – and soon after we landed he said, 'We'll all meet in the hotel bar and get on with it.'

When I went down that evening, a group of the lads was already there – Charlie, Viv, our goalkeeper John Lukic and 'Rodders' (Tony Adams) – and there were a load of bottles on the bar. We then started to play a drinking word game called Fizz Buzz where, if you got it wrong, you had to take a drink, a 'finger' of a spirit. Pretty soon, I was in an argument with Charlie. He said the forfeit I had drunk of three 'fingers' should have been four and I had to do it again. That would have meant me drinking seven 'fingers' in a matter of moments, so I said, 'Bollocks – I'm not doing it.' Then it got a little heated and it became a test of who was going to back down.

He called me a wanker or something like that and threw his drink over me, so I told him what to do and threw my drink over him. Viv was as good as gold and stepped in to calm things down before they got out of hand.

That night seven or eight of us set off into Albufeira for a bit of fun and ended up in a nightclub. Charlie was the star and word soon got round that the Arsenal players were in, and a group of girls who were in talking to some American marines dumped them for us. There was a bit of kerfuffle as a result, so we told the Americans to fuck off and there was a lot of 'see you', 'no, see you' – the usual stuff in a nightclub. Eventually, we walked out of the disco, thinking nothing about it. But that was just the start.

Four of the marines came out and called us 'fucking English trash', and then they jumped in a small hire car and drove it at us as we were walking across the road. Our reserve goalkeeper Rhys Wilmot tried to kick the car but missed. They missed us too, thank God, but reversed and started coming back at us again. Charlie just happened to have a vodka bottle in his hand, as you do, and he threw it at the car's windscreen. Both the bottle and the windscreen shattered, and their car crashed into the kerb.

When your adrenaline is going, it's either fight or flee – so we fled. We got back to the hotel at about 4 or 5am and thought that was that – just an ordinary night out, really.

The next day, we were all gathered in the hotel bar ready to go out on the razzle again when three policemen came in and went up to reception. We didn't think it was anything to do with us until three of the marines got out of the police van outside, walked into the hotel and pointed us out. They said, 'Him, him and him,' and eventually pointed at six of us. We asked what it was all about and we gathered that the marines had made some complaint or other. Charlie, Viv and Rhys were singled out and had to go with the police, and three of the rest of us went with them for support. We thought it was all a bit of a joke and that after it was all sorted out we'd soon be let out and back at the hotel.

While all this was going on, George Graham and the rest of the coaching staff were out playing golf, blissfully ignorant of what was happening back in town. Someone at the hotel thought it would be a good idea to let him know what was going on and phoned him up at the golf club. He was on the 17th tee about to sink a putt when he got a message: 'Mr Graham, half your team have been arrested.' Needless to say, he was not best pleased.

As he and Theo headed towards the police station, we were getting worried. None of us spoke Portuguese, they weren't speaking in English and it was very hard to understand what was going on. Eventually, the police chief came in and, in broken English, announced, 'We are going to charge you with attempted murder.'

What?!!

Viv Anderson had been involved in these discussions and, as soon as the policemen said this, I swear I saw a black man go white. All the colour really seemed to drain from his face. Eventually, he managed to compose himself enough to say to this senior officer, 'We want to see whoever is in charge.'

It didn't do much good as the man simply replied, 'I am.'

Eventually, the Boss turned up with someone from the hotel to help interpret as we were insisting that no one had thrown anything and that the car windscreen must have smashed when the marines crashed the car. Eventually, it emerged that they wanted money to cover the damage to the car. Charlie then said, 'How much? I'll sort it.' It turned out it was in the region of £2,000. We managed to get back to the hotel and Charlie went up to his room and came back with £2,000 in cash! I thought, Top man, Charlie.

Before we all got too carried away with his generosity, however, he also said, 'Give me £300 each when we get back.'

I hoped he might forget about it, so when we got home I didn't pay him for two weeks. Then he asked me for the money so I had to cough it up. Well, he is a Jock, after all.

8

There's nothing like a local derby to get the fans' blood going. You can keep Rangers–Celtic, Liverpool–Everton and the rest – give me a north London game any time.

The rivalry dates back to just before World War I, when Arsenal moved from their original home south of the river at Woolwich because they needed to expand. A site in Highbury was chosen as there was room to build a stadium – and Tottenham Hotspur immediately put the boot in. They objected to the plan, saying the area shouldn't have two sides only about three miles apart, but they lost. Gooners fans reckon they have been losing ever since.

So, when we got drawn against them in the two legs of the Littlewoods Cup semi-final in February 1987, we all knew there would be two hard games ahead. Spurs, who were managed at that time by David Pleat, had a side that was packed with internationals: Glenn Hoddle, Chris Waddle, Ossie Ardiles, Ray

Clemence and the like, and the Allen cousins, Paul and Clive. They were good going forwards, but they weren't so good at the back.

Charlie Nicholas was up front for us for the first leg at Highbury and I was playing on the right wing. We were a goal down at half-time as Clive Allen had scored for them just before the break, but in the second half I almost put us level when I got the ball about 30 yards out and volleyed it. Clemence was beaten and it would have been the goal of all time, but it hit the bar so no one remembers it. As it was, we ended up losing by the only goal of the match, our first defeat at Highbury under George Graham.

It was another three weeks before the second leg at White Hart Lane and this time I was ruled out by injury. Clive Allen was again a pain, because he scored for them in the first half so at the interval we were 2–0 down over the tie. Then they made a big mistake.

As George was giving us his talk, we could hear Spurs fans' Chas and Dave song 'Ossie's on his way to Wembley' blaring out over the loudspeakers. Then we heard some Tottenham official's voice coming over the tannoy saying, 'Tickets for Wembley will be available...' They were already giving the crowd details of how to get their big-match tickets. Bang out of order! George didn't bother going on about tactics – he just said, 'Do you need any more motivation?' The answer was a resounding no.

We were on fire after that, and Viv Anderson and Niall Quinn got the second-half goals that meant we won on the night. There was no 'away goals count double' rule then, so we had to go through 30 minutes of extra-time before it ended all square. We lost the toss for the venue of the third and deciding game, so it would be back to White Hart Lane a few days later for the showdown in front of a crowd of 41,000 to see who would play Liverpool at Wembley.

Yet again, it was Clive Allen who scored for Spurs, his 39th goal in 38 games that season, and, as it was well into the game, the 62nd minute, we had to come back from the dead once more. We were practically in the coffin this time, as there were only eight minutes left when my old Colchester teammate Ian Allinson, who'd come on as sub, equalised, but after that there was only going to be one winner. Sure enough, Rocky, David Rocastle, scored in injury time to give us victory in a three-match saga that had seen us 'beaten' several times.

This was a massive result for Arsenal, a real turnaround for the club. It was our first final since the 1979 FA Cup game eight years earlier when Alan Sunderland had got that late winner against Manchester United. And we hadn't got to the final of this competition since 1969, when it was known as the League Cup. We were at Wembley! The one drawback for me was that I'd been injured, and as there was now only a month before the final I was worried that I might not get back into the side.

One thing I wasn't going to miss out on, however, was my final tickets and the unofficial bonuses that went with them – black-market sales. My free allocation was 24 tickets, but I was also allowed to buy 96 at their face value, ranging from £10 standing to £40 or £50 in the good seats. Every club has a go-between for these sales and at that time it was one of our first-team players. I didn't need to ask twice about what would happen next: I knew where the vast majority of the tickets would end up – with Stan Flashman.

Now, for those of you too young to remember, I'll give you a brief introduction to the life and times of 19-stone 'Fat' Stan Flashman. He was the son of an East End tailor and started his working life selling pots and pans in Houndsditch. He soon packed that in when he went to a Spurs' home match one day and saw how much the touts were making outside the ground and reckoned that was the life for him. He bought some tickets there and then and quickly sold them on to some supporters. He made £40 that afternoon, which is what it took him a week to earn normally, and a new career was born.

Stan, who liked to be known as a 'ticket broker', became king of the touts and boasted he could get tickets for anything: from a Cup Final to a Buckingham Palace garden party – they were all fair game for him. He even boasted he'd sold black-market tickets for Princess Anne's wedding. He was continually being exposed by the newspapers over his ticket deals, but he didn't seem to mind. He probably reckoned that it was all good publicity for the business.

Bizarrely, at the time I had my dealings with him, he was also chairman of Barnet FC. He had rescued them and was in charge as they went from non-league football to league status. His manager there was the colourful Barry Fry, whom he sacked at least 20 times during their period together, although Fry would usually just ignore the sacking and turn up for work the next day.

So it was no surprise when the first-team squad member in charge of selling the tickets – I can't name him because he is still involved in professional football – took me up to Stan's big house in leafy Totteridge in north London to discuss some business. Stan met us in his vest and braces and said, 'Come in,' and then I was introduced to him. 'Is he all right?' he asked, looking at me. He wasn't enquiring about my health – he wanted reassurance that I could be trusted.

'Yes,' said my mate, so that was the first hurdle out of the way.

We went into the front room and his wife Helen was sitting there. She turned to her husband and said, 'Stan, are you ready for your prawns?' He said he was, and as we made ourselves comfortable she went into the kitchen and came back with the biggest plate of prawns I have ever seen in my life. It looked as though they had taken every prawn in the North Sea and put it on that plate for Stan's snack.

As he started shovelling them down, there was some unfinished business to take care of. 'How much do I owe you?' asked Stan.

'It's about £500 to £600,' said my pal.

Stan put down his massive plate of prawns and walked into a small box room. I noticed he had a fridge in there, which seemed strange, but then he opened the fridge door and I couldn't believe what I saw. It was packed with money. I had never seen so much cash in my life. There was no food or drink in there – there wasn't room for it – just banknotes. Perhaps Stan thought that if he was burgled the bad guys wouldn't look in a fridge. Perhaps it was handy, or perhaps he just liked his money cold! Either way I will always remember Stan's hiding place.

Stan took out a pile and handed it over, obviously in payment for services rendered in the past, and the first part of the transaction was complete. We then asked Stan what sort of price we could be looking at for the Littlewoods Cup game. Stan reckoned one and a half times on top of face value, so a £20 ticket, for example, would fetch £50. 'I wouldn't normally get that for the Littlewoods Cup,' Stan said, 'but as you're playing Liverpool there won't be as many tickets flying around in London.'

It worked out that the players would probably make between £3,000 and £3,500 each from the deal, and most of the lads took part. I didn't make as much as the rest of them, because I decided to hire a coach for all my friends and relatives in Colchester to see the game. I gave them the best seats too and let my cheaper tickets go to Stan. I think I only pocketed about £800 in total.

The procedure was very simple: the go-between handed the money over at the training ground in brown paper envelopes the day after collecting the payout from Stan. It all seemed too simple – and too good – to be true. Sure enough, it was.

Three months into the next season, I got a call from George Graham saying he and the club's managing director Ken Friar wanted to see me at 2pm. I asked Theo what it was about and he said he had no idea. So I went into the office and there were the two of them, looking very serious. I said, 'What's this about, Mr Friar?'

'We are disappointed in you, Perry,' he replied. 'One of your tickets has been found by the FA to have been sold on the black market.'

Oops! What had happened was the FA, as usual, had checked on some tickets and obviously the clubs had kept a record of which player had got which tickets, so they had been able to run it down to me.

'This is not looking good for you or the club,' Ken Friar went on. 'The FA are going to take disciplinary action.'

I thought, I'm not going to be the lamb to the slaughter on this one, so I told them I'd given the ticket to a mate who must have sold it. A week later, I got a letter from Ken Friar saying that the FA needed a name and address of the person who got the ticket. No problem: I just told them it was Mandy's cousin Mick and gave them his full name and address. The outcome of it all was that he ended up being banned from matches at Wembley for five years! How pathetic. How would anyone know who he was anyway?

Incidentally, all that wheeling and dealing didn't do Stan Flashman much good in the end. At one stage, his Barnet players threatened to strike because they weren't being paid, and the

Inland Revenue investigated financial irregularities at the club. Why, for example, did their near-9,000-capacity ground look full, when records said there were only 4,881 spectators in there? He only escaped their clutches by being declared unfit to plead on physical- and mental-health grounds, and he was eventually declared bankrupt. Before his death in 1999, he was reduced to living in a semi in Ilford. I can't help but wonder what he kept in the fridge there...

9

And so the big day itself dawned, 5 April 1987. Arsenal against Liverpool at Wembley on a sunny Sunday in front of a packed house – including those there courtesy of Stan Flashman and his dodgy tickets – and millions watching on TV.

We hadn't been doing so well in the run-up to the match. Our challenge for the title had lost ground and we'd been knocked out of the FA Cup – 3–1 at home by Watford, of all teams. The Boss had arranged to buy Alan Smith from Leicester for £750,000 to play up front, but 'Smudge' wasn't leaving them until their relegation battle was over one way or the other, so he didn't figure in the team selection. Even so, I still reckoned I had an uphill struggle as the side was set in stone, despite those poor results in the run-up to the match.

Nowadays, it's commonplace to have first-team squads of 19, 20 or more and rotate them, both to keep everyone happy and to gee up the players who start with the knowledge that their place isn't secure. As far as George Graham was concerned, though, the only place rotation that took place was in his carefully tendered garden. He didn't believe in chopping and changing a side, which is why some players would practically have to have a broken leg before they said they weren't fit to play. They knew that once they'd lost their place it would be a hell of a job to get it back.

I'd already sussed that Michael Thomas was probably going to be one of the two subs and I just hoped I would be the other. As fate would have it, the other main contender was Ian Allinson, the other Colchester boy, but the Boss named me. It was fantastic, absolutely fantastic. I'd started the season at Colchester playing in front of practically no one, and here I was eight months later going to Wembley in front of a crowd of 92,000.

We were massive underdogs for the game, even though we were fairly high in the table. The reason was simple: our opponents were the mighty Liverpool, a team full of players who were used to big matches – and winning them. This was Arsenal's first final in years and half our team had never played at Wembley. Liverpool practically lived there – it was their eighth final appearance in ten years.

Liverpool were in that 19-year period of their history that saw them only once finish out of the top two in the league. They were the current League Champions and, although they actually finished in second place behind Everton in season 1986–87, they regained the title the next year. Liverpool had the habit of beating all-comers in Europe as well and, but for the ban on English sides, would probably have been continuing that tradition too.

They also had players like Ian Rush, Alan Hansen and Bruce

Grobbelaar in their line-up, so the bookies were in no doubt as to who they thought would win. But George Graham was ready for them.

As always, we stayed at the Noke Hotel in St Albans and we went down for the team talk on the Sunday morning. Paul Merson wasn't playing, but he wanted to video the talk with his camera. A pity he didn't. The Boss got out his flip-chart and systematically went through their side one by one – and these were some of the best players in the world, let alone England.

Grobbelaar – 'Prone to lapses,' said the Boss.

Hansen – 'Looks great and elegant at the back, but takes too many chances. Hustle him and he will make mistakes.'

Rush – 'Is his heart going to be in it? He's gone off the boil.'

Now that verdict was the best of all. The Boss was actually a huge admirer of Ian Rush and his goalscoring, but was telling us that as Rush was heading for Juventus – where he later said he didn't settle because Italy was 'like a foreign country' – his mind wouldn't be on the job in hand.

All this took about 20 minutes, and at the end of it I reckoned we'd got a great chance. It was brilliant tactics by the Boss. He'd run through this side, who everyone else was in awe of, and taken them apart. In truth, he probably knew better than anyone what fine players they were, but he gave us the belief that we could beat them.

It hadn't been all that long ago that I had been a ball boy at Wembley, but this was so different. As we walked out on the pitch through that famous tunnel, the noise seemed 20 times louder than I remembered it. I was looking up for my mates and my family – I couldn't believe it was all happening.

As the subs, Michael Thomas and I were fairly relaxed as we sat down and started to enjoy the game. It was a half-decent match for once – normally Wembley games disappoint – but from an Arsenal point of view it took a bad turn when Ian Rush scored in the 24th minute. It was his 36th goal of the season – so much for 'gone off the boil'.

Perhaps more importantly, he had scored in 145 previous games for Liverpool and they had never lost one of them. If we were to beat them, we'd have to make history. Well, it didn't take long for us to start doing just that. A Paul Davis free-kick wasn't cleared and Charlie Nicholas was on hand to scramble home Viv Anderson's cross. Game on.

Mickey Thomas was sent on to replace Martin Hayes on what was turning into a very hot day, and with about 20 minutes left the Boss decided to bring off Niall Quinn, so he turned to me and said, 'Warm up, Grovesy.' At the same time, Liverpool decided to bring one of their lads off the bench to replace Paul Walsh – a certain Kenny Dalglish. So there we were, yours truly from Colchester alongside the Liverpool player-manager, a legend in the game and one of the finest British players of all time. You could almost hear everyone watching thinking that Liverpool were bringing on a quality player, and Arsenal were bringing on... who exactly?

The Boss gave me brief straightforward instructions as I prepared to enter the arena – 'Just run in behind them. They're knackered.'

I'd only been on the pitch a few moments when Kenny Sansom cleared a ball down the line and I set off down the left flank. Gary Gillespie came across to take me out but I slipped it under him and I was away. As the man from *The Times* wrote the next day, 'Groves drifted past Gillespie and drove the ball towards the near post.'

The reason for that was simple. I'd got near the box and if I'd been coming in from the right I'd have shot. As it was, I didn't feel so confident and I saw Charlie coming into the box, so I squared it to him. Next thing it was in the net – he'd scored. Simple as that. Going back to the halfway line, I thought, I've made my mark here, all right!

I think the game only lasted another 18 minutes or so, but they were the longest 18 minutes of my life. Normally, I couldn't tackle a fish supper, but for the rest of the game I didn't make a mistake when it came to tackles. There was one 50–50 ball between me and their Danish midfield player Jan Molby, who looked about twice my size. But I just took him and the ball and as he hit the ground I was off and running.

When the final whistle blew, the place erupted. It was silly-hat time with a Pearly King-style cap, the Cup on my head and red-and-white scarves around my neck. You're meant to do a lap of honour at the end, but I think I did five. In the dressing room it was champagne everywhere and someone gave us replicas of the Littlewoods Cup to keep. You also had two shirts, one that you wore with grass stains and all that stuff on it that you swapped, and one that you kept. I kept the one I'd worn and swapped the one I didn't wear and I ended up with King Kenny's shirt.

Then it was really party time. Graham Rix had booked a restaurant in Southgate in north London, so we all headed there. It was a pity but Charlie, who'd scored both goals, couldn't make it, as he had family come down from Scotland to watch the match and he was going out with them.

Paul Davis – one of our three black players with David Rocastle and Michael Thomas who we nicknamed the Three Degrees – had invited actor Tom Watt, Lofty from *EastEnders* – and he was sitting at our table. I thought he was just one of those fashionable supporters – a celebrity Gooner – and I said to Paul Merson, 'Look at him, Merse – jumping on the bandwagon.' There was a character called Lou Beale on the programme at the time who would say to Watt, 'Well, Lofty...' so me and Merse kept calling that out – 'Well, Lofty' this and 'Well, Lofty' that. I don't know what the bloke must have thought but after two hours he left.

I later found out that, far from being someone who'd jumped on the bandwagon, he was a real Gooner – Arsenal through and through. I met him later and realised how much the club meant to him, so I'm glad he'd joined us – even though I had taken the piss out of him.

Eventually, I drove Mandy home to her mum and dad's in Colchester where we were staying. As we got near their house, we were stopped by a police patrol car. Oh no, a crap end to the perfect day. I wasn't legless but I had been drinking and so I feared the worst. The policeman recognised me and asked how far I'd got to go. I told him the truth: I was about one mile from home. Then he said, 'You've had a nice day, let's not ruin it,' let me go and even followed me to my door just to make sure nothing happened. If only every day could be like that, eh?

The season sort of petered out after that. As I've said, our league form had gone off a bit, and soon after Wembley we lost 3–1 at West Ham United. Just to rub it in, there were a couple of Highbury old boys in the Hammers side. Stewart Robson hadn't played much under George and had lost his place to Steve Williams, so he'd moved to Upton Park a few months earlier. Even worse, one of the Hammers' goals was scored by Liam Brady, a genuine Gooners legend who'd returned to English football after several seasons in Italy.

The Boss had played me and Charlie up front against West Ham and it wasn't a success. You could describe it as Laurel and Hardy or perhaps Abbott and Costello. The truth was it was more like Laurel and Costello – it didn't work at all. At least Charlie could take comfort in the fact he got a new deal with the club, a year's contract. The Boss loved his ability, but his work rate wasn't what he wanted. Still, he'd scored twice at Wembley, so he signed for another 12 months.

We ended up finishing fourth in the league and then had a pretty eventful end-of-season break in Cyprus.

Faced with the summer off, I thought I'd go and see the Boss about my wages. I thought I'd done well, so I went to his office and he said, 'What can I do for you, Grovesy?'

So I told him I was looking for some more money.

He said, 'You've done well, but not well enough. You could be a flash in the pan and there is a lot in your game that you should work on. I can't go to the board for more money for you after you've only been here five minutes – they'll think I'm mad. Do it for me in the next three or four months and perhaps we'll think about it then.'

'That's not great motivation, is it?' I said.

'Well, that's it,' he replied. 'Goodbye. Have a good summer.'

I drove home thinking, You tight Scots bastard – it's not your money...

10

I got married in the close season – 20 June 1987, to be precise – at St Andrew's Church in Colchester to Mandy Farrell, who I'd been going out with since my Colchester United days.

Our romance had started in a slightly unusual fashion, as you might expect if I'm involved. Mandy used to come and watch her brother Andy play for Colchester when I was in the side. She was attractive, aged about 20 or 21, and a virgin. In that part of the world, that's like finding a Penny Black, I can tell you. I ended up spending a lot of time at her family home, on the face of it seeing a lot of Andy but really wanting to get near his sister. She didn't want to go out with me, though, because she had a mate called Jane who fancied me and she didn't want to upset her. But I wore her down in the end.

Mandy was a domestic assistant at a maternity home in Colchester and I used to call her a 'pooper scooper' because of her job. When the 'U's were at home, she would come to watch

Andy play and stand behind the goal with her mate Jane, so in the warm-up before one game I kicked the ball towards her and went to get it back. But I'd hidden a pair of knickers down my shorts and when I got near I got them out and shouted at her, 'Oi, you left something in my car last night!' and threw them at her. The crowd parted like the Red Sea and they landed at her feet. Smooth or what?

Even though she was quiet while I was brash, we eventually started going out in the Datsun Cherry I had bought. She was a 'nice girl', though, and it took a while for the ginga to strike!

In the run-up to the wedding, one of my first girlfriends had written to me at Arsenal saying how proud she was of me and perhaps we could meet up. She was living in north London at the time and it didn't take me long to agree to that. I met her in Covent Garden one Tuesday after training and she looked fantastic, so one thing led to another. While I was with her on the first meeting, I phoned the man who was to be my best man, Chris 'Chinney' Heard, and said, 'Guess who I'm with?' At first, he thought it was some of the Arsenal players, but I told him the truth and said, 'It's a blast from the past.' I saw her two or three times before the marriage and I don't think she wanted me to go through with it, but that was never in question.

On the big day itself, I managed to mess a couple of things up. We had been away for a cruise beforehand, so there was no honeymoon as such, so we were to spend our wedding night in a hotel. Unfortunately, I didn't get round to organising the honeymoon suite until the Wednesday before the ceremony, so by that time it was already booked. I had to settle for an ordinary double room with a bottle of champagne in it.

On the morning of the big day, I was lying in the bath and Chinney was busy around the house. Suddenly, I shouted at the top of my voice, 'I can't go through with it!' He came in to see what was the matter and I said, all serious, 'I can't go through with it.'

He really believed me and went into a panic. 'What am I going to say?' he said. 'All the people will be there, I'll have to apologise. What am I going to say?'

I couldn't keep it up much longer, though, so I told him I was only joking.

We had time for a couple of drinks before the ceremony and afterwards it was back to Shrub End village hall for the reception, complete with Caribbean steel band and a disco. We could have got somewhere better but I wanted it to be there with about 140 people, all family and friends, no hangers-on. I remember I got booed as I was making my speech – no change there then.

Between about 4.30 and 7pm, there is always a lull in these sort of things, so all my football mates went down the Leather Bottle pub near by. I asked where they had gone and when I found out I thought I might as well join them. I didn't think anyone would miss me, but after about an hour one of Mandy's aunts came and dragged me back by the ear.

I'd also forgotten to book a cab to take us back to the hotel after the reception and as it was a Saturday we had to wait until about half-past-midnight before Mandy's family came back to pick us up. We ended up filling the time by helping the caretaker sweep up, me in my tails and Mandy in her wedding dress.

It was about this time that the first references to me started to appear in fanzines, complete with mentions of my Tintin haircut. Chinney's missus Dawn used to cut my hair and she had got rid of my mullet. Then Sue English, the wife of another pal, Tom English of Colchester United, gave me the Tintin style. I had natural curls so she just shaved it at the sides. I put gel on top, as all the players did, but I reckon one tube used to last me about three years. I thought I looked the dog's bollocks.

Some of the references to me were funny, some of them were personal. One of them said that I used to run as though I had a Mars Bar up my arse, things like that. I also wore the short shorts that all the other players had, but mine looked shorter because of my massive arse. It was the first time I'd been mentioned as being something special to the fans – one way or another – and it was a taste of things to come.

After a short break in Tenerife with Mandy and Tony Adcock and his wife, I reported back for training and the season 1987–88 was about to begin.

Now everyone thinks of Arsenal as super-fit, but I always thought the training was a piece of piss really. I was used to running eight, nine, ten miles at Colchester, but when we started the pre-season at Trent Park in north London we would never run for more than four minutes at a time. We would go through the woods and I would think, We're not getting fit here.

The Gaffer would tell us that he came to Trent Park to run on Sunday mornings himself and we would say, 'No wonder you look so fit, Gaffer,' but we'd be taking the piss. He wasn't called Gorgeous George for nothing and we knew he was proud of his appearance. He was also known as 'Stroller' when he played, and we reckoned that he did more running as a manager than he ever did when he was playing.

Most clubs do a 12-minute run – eight or nine laps around the pitch – but at Arsenal we just jogged and then sprinted, jogged then sprinted. But when the season started I felt really sharp even though they were the easiest pre-seasons I have ever done. George's big thing was 'You have to run with style', maintaining that if you did that it was more efficient, so in spite of those 'easy' training sessions we were as fit as anyone.

Before the first game of the year started, the Boss took us away to Largs in Scotland for the week to train and prepare for the season. We didn't think much of where we were based and four or five of the players went to see George to complain about the facilities, but all he said was, 'You are here to work.'

But there was absolutely nothing to do after work, and there was a curfew for the week – 'be in bed by ten' and all that stuff. One night, though, the Boss let us go into the town of Largs for the evening, but we had to be in by 11.30pm. There was me, Graham Rix, our reserve keeper Rhys Wilmot, Charlie Nicholas and Paul Merson. The train-spotters all decided to stay in.

So we were in a pub and it got to 11.20pm, and as it was a 20-minute walk back we were obviously going to be late. Merse and I were the youngest so we couldn't bail out – we had to wait for the others. When we did get back to where we were staying at 12.15am, Theo Foley was waiting for us and said, 'Morning, gentlemen.'

The next morning, George called a team meeting and said, 'Five of you were late – I saw you,' even though he hadn't, he had just been told about it. 'The five of you know who you are and you are all fined £100 because you broke the curfew. If it happens again you are out.' Then he took me and Merse to one side and said, 'You two are mixing with the wrong people.' I got the message – you don't look a gift horse in the mouth.

One day up there, we went for a walk and there was one of our more senior players, a happily married man as they say, sitting under a tree in the middle of nowhere, very close to a young lady who wasn't his wife. You should have seen his face. After that, at training we all began singing, 'Don't sit under the apple tree, with anyone else but me...' and he was terrified for ages that what he'd been up to would come out.

We also played some practice games up in Scotland and after one of them I phoned my dad for a chat. One of my rivals for a forward role was David Rocastle, who was a little bit younger than me. Now Rocky was a terrific player and one of the nicest men in football, but of course I wanted his place. So after this game where I didn't think he'd played well, I said to Dad, 'It's between me and Rocky, and he had a stinker.' I put the phone down, turned around, and there was Rocky.

He took it well though and just said, 'You weren't so sharp yourself when you came on.' Some guys might have made more of it, but not Rocky.

The week ended all right, as we played Celtic in front of about 35,000 people at their Parkhead ground: we won 5–1 and I scored. Back home, I started the season off as sub but after about five or six games the Boss brought me in. We won 6–0 at home to Portsmouth but I got the hump because I didn't score, even though we'd won easily.

I scored my first goal of the season at Doncaster in the Littlewoods (League) Cup when we won 3–0, and then we beat Chelsea 3–1 at Highbury to go top of the league. We were there or thereabouts as the Christmas holiday games approached and it was time to play Portsmouth again. I had one of the worst games of my life – it was a nightmare. And when I had a nightmare I didn't try and hide, so it really did look terrible. Noel Blake was marking me for Portsmouth – and I made him look good!

I was up front with Niall Quinn and at half-time George went through everyone in the team. Then he turned to us and said, 'See you two, you have five minutes or you get the hook.' He lied

– he brought us off after four and a half. Alan Smith and Merse were sent on and we equalised to get out of it 1–1.

There were certain players, such as Tony Adams or Rocky, who might have two or three bad games but would keep their places. But I knew that if I had a dodgy half or 60 minutes then I might be off or dropped for the next game. I was always playing under that pressure. If the team was winning, it helped, but if we drew or lost I'd be bombed.

I was on the subs bench when we played Millwall – the Boss's old club – at home in the third round of the FA Cup in January. There was a lot of police there for crowd trouble – we had the biggest gate of the day at 42,083 – but also to stop a crime – the Millwall fans were plotting to steal the clock from the Clock End. How they hoped to do it I don't know. It was about seven metres wide, made of marble and 80ft off the ground. As I was warming up, I noticed there were four policemen below it keeping an eye on it, though I never could work out how they thought it would get nicked. As for the game, we won it 2–0.

We also won away at Sheffield Wednesday in the quarter-finals of the Littlewoods Cup that January in a game I remember for different reasons. I was on the bench again and it was a cold Yorkshire night: I was freezing and couldn't even feel my toes. The game had 0–0 written all over it – they could have played for ten years and no one would have scored. I certainly didn't want to go out there, and then, with about 20 minutes to go, Nigel Winterburn, out of desperation, had a shot from about 30 yards.

It pea-rolled along the ground and a little mole must have popped up from the grass and waved at someone just as their goalkeeper Martin Hodge went to stop the shot, and into the net it went. I leaped up in the air in excitement but forgot I was deep inside the dug-out. As a result I hit my head on the iron bar that ran along its roof and knocked myself unconscious. Everyone else on the bench had gone forward and then up in the air, so they were all right and celebrating on the side of the pitch. I had just gone straight up and hit my head. The Sheffield Wednesday fans who saw me were laughing their heads off, even though their team had just let a goal in.

When the Boss and the rest of the bench calmed down, they came back to the dug-out but none of them noticed me. A little while later, the Boss told Gary Lewin to get me warmed up, but when Gary saw me he realised there was a problem. He came out with a line you don't hear too often in football: 'The sub's unconscious.' I came round and went on as sub for Niall Quinn, but I had a bump on my head like some cartoon character.

A few weeks earlier, the Boss had called me in and put my money up to £700 a week basic, plus another year on my contract which meant I had three years on it now. I also got a £5,000 disturbance allowance as he'd told me he wanted me to move nearer London. So I bought a four-bedroomed house in a modern mews in Stanway in Colchester – all of seven miles nearer Highbury – and pocketed the money, thank you. I'd bought myself a Montego and Mandy was only working part-time at the maternity home, as I was earning good money now.

Before our next big match, the first leg of a Littlewoods Cup tie against Everton at Goodison on a Sunday in February, we went away for four or five days 'bonding' in Marbella. I'll tell you everything that happened on the trip later, but we returned on the Friday and trained on the Saturday. That training took the form of a 25-minute game against the youth team and they beat us 2–0! We were so heavy-legged we were crap. We sat in the changing rooms and thought, We are going to get hammered.

After we travelled up to Liverpool, I thought it might relax things if I played a little joke on Kevin Richardson, who I was sharing a room with. I told all the other lads to keep him talking while I went and hid in the wardrobe in our room. I stayed in there for about 30–35 minutes and began to think it was a double bluff – perhaps the others had told him what I was doing and they were going to leave me in there. But then he did come up to the room and, as he walked in, in darkness, I leaped out and shouted 'Ha!' at him, just like Burt Kwouk does to Peter Sellers in the *Pink Panther* movies. Kevin immediately went into a ju-jitsu pose to defend himself, only to realise it was me. 'You fuckin' ginger twat!'

The game was live on television and Everton were really flying then with players like Graham Sharp, Gary Stevens, Trevor Steven and Pat van den Hauwe in their side. But after just ten minutes we took the lead when I hit a left-foot volley past Neville Southall, their Welsh international goalie. Southall was such a good keeper that if you put one past him it practically counted as two, and as the game went on I hoped that there would be no more scoring (there wasn't), as I wanted to have all the headlines to myself.

It's a pity that they didn't show goals on television as often in those days as they do now when they're repeated all the time. Otherwise, people would still think I was better than I really was!

11

One of the biggest football rivalries in recent years has been between Arsenal and Manchester United. It isn't just that they are two top teams always in the running for trophies, there has been genuine bad blood between the clubs. And I reckon a lot of it can be traced back to one game I played in.

We'd just had that major win over Everton at Goodison when United came to us for an FA Cup Fifth Round match. Highbury was packed with 54,000 fans. United had internationals like Viv Anderson, who'd left us for Old Trafford, Steve Bruce, Gordon Strachan, Brian McClair and Norman Whiteside in their team, while I was up front alongside Alan Smith.

It was a fantastic match. Smudge put us in front with a header and then Mike Duxbury headed into his own goal. McClair got one back for them just after half-time and after that they really came for us. Eventually, they got a penalty in the 87th minute after the referee thought Michael Thomas had tripped Whiteside, but Whiteside had conned the referee. McClair took the kick in front of the North Bank – and promptly hit it high over the bar. Nigel Winterburn was so pleased that he ran around McClair, taunting him. I suppose it wasn't too clever, but it summed up what we felt towards each other, and it was to come to the boil again pretty soon.

A few days later, we had the second leg of the Littlewoods (League) Cup semi-final against Everton. Perhaps this was the best game I ever played, certainly for all 90 minutes. We won 3–1 in front of another crowd of over 50,000 and I had a hand in all our three goals. I even put Martin Hayes through to win a penalty, although he missed it.

That night we all went into London to celebrate and there was a bar near the Café de Paris with a gigantic screen showing highlights of the match. The place was packed with birds and there I was on the screen – talk about 'Tonight I am going to be Brad Pitt...'

At the start of March, we were at home to Tottenham, now managed by George Graham's big mate Terry Venables, in the league – our fourth massive game in under a month. It was on a Sunday and again live on television and I was playing up front.

In the first half, I went through on a one-on-one, but the ball sat up and I shanked it completely. I was out on my own and couldn't blame anything – I just shanked it. One newspaper report the next day said I was 'guilty of embarrassing profligacy... he pulled his effort not so much inches as yards wide'. Harsh but fair.

Alan Smith scored to make it 1–0. Then, out of nowhere, Clive Allen scored for them. As the game restarted, I thought I would be crucified if we just drew after missing a sitter. With 15 minutes to go, Kenny Sansom took a throw and it skidded to me.

I took a touch and hit it with my left foot and it flew in: 2–1 to us! Those are the goals that you need to score, because if you end up winning you can then laugh about the one you missed, especially against Spurs. The Boss said afterwards I should have hit the target in the first half – well, I knew *that* – but he also said I was arguably the man of the match.

These days, lots of players practise their celebrations so they can be caught on camera when they score. I never did anything to play up to the camera – I wouldn't be clever enough to get a routine ready. I was always lost in the moment anyway. I used to say that scoring was the next best thing to sex, but sometimes it's better.

So, we had played four gigantic games in under a month and won them all and I'd scored two winners live on TV in front of millions. In football there is no grey. You are either fantastic or shite – there is no in between. One person who will probably agree with that is Paul Gascoigne. We were at home to Newcastle United towards the end of March and he was playing. He wasn't 'Gazza' then, if you get my meaning, but you could tell that he was a special player.

They got a penalty in the eighth minute, and Gazza took it but put it wide. We'd already had a bit of a fracas and as he ran back I could see that he was welling up inside. So I said to him, 'Chins up, big fella.' Then, just to rub it in, I said, 'Oh look, you can retake it.'

He immediately looked round and then saw I was joking. 'You ginger twat,' he said.

Then I scored with a header and, as I ran back, I went past him and said, 'Look, that's how it's done. It's not hard.'

A few minutes after that, the ball bounced in midfield and as I went for it I felt this elbow in my face, nose, everything. It was

Gazza. The match ended 1–1 and I walked over to him to shake hands but he didn't even want to make eye contact. I thought, He's just a kid, he'll have to grow up.

After I'd changed, I saw the press wanted to talk to me, but all they wanted to talk about was the elbow incident. I said, 'He has great ability – he doesn't need to go around elbowing people. If he loses it, it could ruin his career, and that would be a shame.' He probably thought, Why doesn't he shut the fuck up? but what I said was quite prophetic, wasn't it?

It was around this time, April 1988, that I came across another man who was to become a soccer legend. We went down to Southampton and, as usual, the Boss started going through their team. We were expecting their Irish international centre-forward Colin Clarke to be playing, but his name was missing and there was an unknown in his place. 'The centre-forward is a young kid making his debut,' said George. 'Alan Shearer. Shearer... Shearer... anyone know anything about him?'

There was a silence until someone mentioned he might have played for an England Under-19 side. In that case, we had a spy in the camp as Paul Merson had also played for them, so he should know all about him. George wasn't panicking – that wasn't his style – but you could see he didn't like sending his team out against someone he had no knowledge of. So he turned to Merse, who wasn't in the line-up that day. 'Merse,' he said, 'what do you know about him?'

We all paid close attention as Merse gave us his run-down on the youngster we'd soon be facing. 'He is not a natural goalscorer,' he said. 'He runs the channels well, holds the ball up well and is quite strong. But he is not a box player.'

'That's great,' George said. 'Thanks, Merse.'

Ninety minutes later, the Boss wasn't in such a good mood.

Seventeen-year-old Alan Shearer had become the first player to score a hat-trick on his full debut in the 100-year history of the First Division, as far as anyone could tell from the record books. He had certainly become the first player to score three on his debut in England for 21 years that afternoon.

Before he retired, Shearer would become the most expensive footballer in the world and score 379 goals in his career – 30 for England and 260, a record, in the Premiership. We had just seen him notch the first three in our 4–2 defeat and George was not a happy bunny. We all went into the dressing room and sat down and waited for it to happen. George put one of his feet on one of the benches and carefully began to shine his shoe. It was not a good sign. I thought the whole thing was hilarious, but I didn't dare let on.

'Where is he?' the Boss asked. We didn't need to be told who he was looking for. There was silence – and certainly no sign of Merse. That was because he was hiding in the showers. 'Merse, are you taking the piss?' George went on. 'Where is he?' He then added – as if he needed to – 'Remind me never to send him on a scouting mission.'

The Boss then walked out and Merse plucked up the courage to appear and put the case for the defence. 'I am not a scout – don't ask me next time.' I don't think the Boss planned to!

Merse was probably my best mate at the Gunners. He was a fantastic footballer with great natural gifts, and he was incredible to be with off the field too. He never did anything by halves, so when he came to talk openly about his problems a few years down the line he admitted he was hooked on drugs, gambling and booze – a full house! He even admitted that with all the rehab meetings he was attending he hardly had any spare time.

I used to call him 'Stanley Unwin' after the comic who appeared on television and always got his words mixed up. Once Merse was reading the newspaper in the dressing room and there was a big story about a siege where the police had armed marksmen on the scene. 'Look,' he said, 'they've got snippers on the roof.'

'They've got what?' I said.

'Snippers,' said Merse. 'They've got snippers everywhere.'

'Oh right,' I said. 'They're going to send hairdressers in with their scissors and combs in case the SAS can't handle it, are they? You mean snipers.'

Then he moved into a house near our London Colney training ground and was moaning because he couldn't put up a satellite dish on the house to watch the sport on Sky. 'The problem is,' he said, 'that we are in the middle of a constellation area.'

'A what?' I said.

'A constellation area.'

'Do you mean Patrick Moore is there looking up at the sky?' I said. 'You mean a conservation area, don't you?'

Merse came up with the answer he often used: 'It's the same thing, isn't it?'

Another time he bought a BMW and somehow spent £5,000 on extras, super CD, tinted windows, special wheels, the lot. 'Look,' he said, pushing some button or other. 'It's got coclining seats.'

'You mean reclining seats,' I said.

'It's the same thing,' came the reply.

Once we flew out from Heathrow and had to meet at the airport very early in the morning. It was around 5.30 or 6am when Merse turned up and said to me, 'I'm dying for a crap,' and headed off to the toilets. There were three signs: 'female', 'male' and 'disabled'. I looked at him and he didn't know what to do. So he turned round to me and said, 'What am I?' He didn't know that 'male' meant man and 'female' meant woman. I said, 'Put your hands in your pockets and feel around for bit and then you'll know.'

It was a season to remember for me for a lot of reasons. Charlie Nicholas had been let go by George early in 1988. He'd sold him to Aberdeen and you can't get much further away from Highbury than that, can you? That meant that I was playing up front quite regularly, with Smudge and Niall Quinn, and Merse was also playing occasionally. It was all going great – but at the end of April the wheels fell off.

We were in the Littlewoods Cup Final at Wembley for the second year running, but this time we were favourites against Luton. Most people expected Steve Williams, our English international midfielder, to be in the side. He'd been out for a while with an injury but had recently got back in the side. Steve is a great guy, but he is one of the most opinionated blokes you could meet. He hammers players, his mates, anyone. He'd even had a go at George some time earlier and had said to him in training, 'Go on, drop me. I'm not bothered. I dare you.' We thought the Gaffer would drop him for the next game but he didn't – but he did drop him for the Littlewoods Cup Final! George says it wasn't because of the row – not much! – but his timing was, shall we say, impeccable.

Luton were still playing their home games on an all-weather pitch and that meant they'd only won three games on grass all season. Also, a month earlier they'd played at Wembley in the Simod Cup, one of those competitions to fill in the gap left by a lack of European matches, but lost to Reading 4–1. So the bookies had us as the big favourites.

We kicked off but for some reason I felt heavy-legged and we had a bad first half. We went in 1–0 behind and George gave me the Portsmouth line: 'You've got five minutes and then you're off.' He lied again – but this time I managed ten minutes.

As I was hauled off, I went past Smudge and got ready to run to the touchline. 'Grovesy,' he said, 'limp!' So I put a little hobble on to make it look as though I'd got a knock. It was still the longest walk of my life as I went across the Wembley turf in front of a packed crowd and millions more watching at home.

Martin Hayes, who replaced me, equalised, but I was glad because that meant there was a chance of a replay and I might be able to do better next time. Then Smudge scored and at 2–1 I didn't mind either. I'd had a stinker, but if we won it meant I'd get a 6 rating in the newspapers instead of the 5 I'd get if we lost, and a winner's medal too.

We could have wrapped it up when Rocky was brought down in the box, but their goalkeeper Andy Dibble saved Nigel Winterburn's penalty. It got worse. With seven minutes left, Luton equalised and then, in the last minute, Brian Stein got the winner for them. If Steve 'Willo' Williams had played I think we would have won.

This was a completely different end of the spectrum from the year before when we'd beaten Liverpool. It was terrible just to look at the other players and the fans. I just wanted to get off quick – I was mortified. We all walked into the dressing room and sat there, hardly saying anything.

Then the Boss, give him his due, came in and said, 'Last year we won in style. This year, let's lose in style,' and got the champagne out. It's funny, though, because no matter how much you drink – champagne, lager, pints, whatever – you can't get pissed after losing on a big occasion like that. Don't ask me why, but there is no way that it seems to affect you. The players had organised a 'do' at the same restaurant as the previous year, but this time it was like a wake. We just weren't in the party mood.

The following Saturday, the only player left out of the first-team squad to play Sheffield Wednesday was... me. The Boss obviously laid much of the blame at my feet. I scored for the reserves but, although we won 2–1 against Spurs, it didn't make up for it. That's football – peaks and troughs.

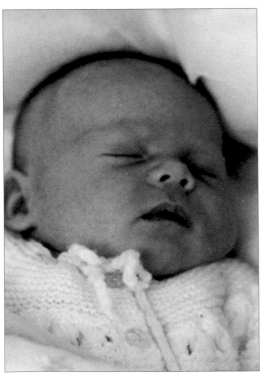

Top: In the beginning... Dad 'Ginge' and mum Patsy.

Bottom left: First known picture of a legend, at two months and already dreaming about the Gooners.

Bottom right: Mum and dad take me on an outing to Victoria Park in Hackney.

Top left: Working on my technique at two – that pitch could do with some reseeding.

Top right: Into Europe at last. On holiday in the Costa del Sol.

Bottom left: Dad and I dressed up for a wedding – *The Sweeney*-style.

Bottom right: Honing up my skills for the Dynamos Under 12s.

Top: With the Dynamos Under 11s. I'm by the shield and our girl 'TV star' player Dawn Lawrence is in the back row, second from right.

Inset: Ouch, that hurt! The ball hit me below the belt and brought tears to my eyes.

Middle: The Dynamos Under 15s. I'm back row, centre and in charge is Mick Brown – or is it Justin from The Darkness?

Left: Collecting my Player of the Year trophy for the Dynamos Under 14s.

The English Schools' Football Association

General Secretary: 4a Eastgate Street, Stafford ST16 2NN.
Tel: 0785 51142

This is to certify that _____ Perry Groves _____

has been registered as an Associated Schoolboy with

_____ Wolverhampton Wanderers _____ Football Club

This registration is subject to the terms of Football League Regulation 45(4)

Registration Number
4000/073

Date of issue _____ 29th May, 1980

General Secretary

Top: Suffolk Schoolboys Under 15s. Five of the team later played professional football. Me, Daryl Godbold (Colchester), third from left, back row; Mark Crowe (Cambridge) fourth left, back row; John Taylor (Luton) front row, right; Tony Spearing (Leicester) third right, front row.

Bottom: Captain, at last. The School Under 15s

Inset: Schoolboy forms with Wolves. Their loss was Arsenal's gain... I think.

Top: The dawn
of the Big Day.
Me and my best
man Chris 'Chinney'
Heard outside
the church.

Left: Me and
Mandy – what a
lovely couple.

Top: April 1983 and I'm strutting my stuff for Colchester against York City. We lost 3–0.

Middle: Local Derby time and it's Colchester United Reserves v Sudbury Town in the Eastern Counties League Final. They don't come much bigger than this! We lost 2–1.

Bottom: A winner. I score from an inch as we beat Southend 2–1 in the FA Cup.

SCHEDULE

a) The Player's employment with the Club began on the ....4th. September..... 19 .86...

b) No employment with a previous employer shall count as part of the Player's continous period of employment hereunder.

c) The Player shall become or continue to be and during the continuance of his employment hereunder shall remain a member of The Football League Players' Benefit Scheme (and a member of the .... (in the latter case shall be liable to make such contributions and in each case) .... Pension Scheme) and as such benefits and subject to such conditions as are set out in the definitive Trust Deed or Rules of the Scheme.

d) A contracting out certificate is not in force in respect of the Player's employment under this Agreement.

e) Basic Wage.

£ ....£350 .... per week from .4.9.1986..... to ..30.6.1989 ....

£ .... per week from .... to ....

£ .... per week from .... to ....

£ .... per week from .... to ....

f) Any other provisions:—

In the event of the expiry of the term of his contract without its being renewed the employee agrees that he shall not bring any claim in respect of such expiry under Part V of the Employment Protection (Consolidation) Act 1978 (or any statutory re-enactment or modification thereof).

Incentive Schedule as attached

P.G.

the sum of £150.00 a~~   will be paid in respect
                                             in which the player

                                             ll be paid as a disturbance
                                             rom Ipswich to London and
                                             cover the following:

                                             Fees, Removal Costs etc.

                                             (Player)
                                             (Secretary/Manager/Chairman)

                                             Manager

SCHEDULE OF BONUSES ATTACHED AND REFERRING TO SERVICE AGREEMENT BETWEEN

ARSENAL FC LIMITED

AND _____Perry GROVES._____

DATED _____4. 9. 1986_____

This schedule forms the whole of Paragraph 23 of the said agreement and payments will be made to the Player as and when he qualifies for such bonuses:

1. TALENT BONUS:
   (i) Football League Championship

   (a) £100 in respect of every match drawn, home or away.
       £250 in respect of every match won, home or away.

   (b) Notwithstanding the above, when the position of the team in the Football League is not lower than sixth, then a further bonus of £50 per match drawn and £100 per match won will be paid.

The League tables will be those published on the Sunday immediately following the last Saturday League programme.

   (c) At the end of the Season, the Club will pay Talent Money on the following basis:

       If the Club finishes FIRST: £120 per appearance
       If the Club finishes SECOND: £ 60 per appearance
       If the Club finishes THIRD: £ 40 per appearance
       If the Club finishes FOURTH: £ 20 per appearance

Notwithstanding the above if the Club gains admission to a European competition, having achieved a position lower than fourth in the Football League Table, Talent Money will be paid on the following basis:

       £10 per appearance

   (ii) F A Challenge Cup

   (a) Per appearance:

       3rd Round: £ 120
       4th Round: £ 160
       5th Round: £ 200
       6th Round: £ 260
       Semi-Final: £ 640
       FINAL: £1600

   (b) If the FA Cup is won the sum of £200 per appearance will be paid at the end of the Season, to each Player taking part.

Top: My first contract with Arsenal, 4 September, 1986.

Bottom: My bonus agreement of the same date.

Top: My first big triumph. Celebrating the Littlewoods Cup 2–1 victory over Liverpool at Wembley. I'm in the front row with a hat on.

Middle: Pearly King Perry. Collecting my medal after the Liverpool Wembley victory.

Right: The goal that Perry forgot: the first of two against Manchester City, after which I was concussed and can't remember either.

12

At the end of the 1987–88 season, we were to take part in a six-a-side tournament in Australia. There were three Aussie sides in it, plus three from England – Arsenal, Manchester City and Nottingham Forest. There were ten players in each squad and all the English teams boarded the same plane for the journey Down Under.

It's a long way to Australia, so there were some guidelines for the journey and George told us there would be a 'no drinking' policy during the long flight. Good one! As we boarded the plane, we also saw the other two teams were in comfortable tracksuits while we were dressed as though we were going to an office in our Arsenal blazers, ties, etc., although George did say that we could change on the plane.

But when we got on board we found that George was in first class, so the no-drinking rule went out of the window. At the time there was a story doing the rounds that Australian cricketer

David Boon had set the drinking record for the route by drinking 36 cans of lager on the flight from Australia to England. It sounded impressive but, as we tried to work out our schedule, we reckoned it was a piece of piss – it was only one can of beer every half an hour. What we didn't take into account was cabin pressure and that got to us, so we knocked it on the head after ten cans or so. But we found something else to keep us busy.

We had changed into our tracksuits and Merse produced a little roulette wheel from somewhere. Pretty soon, he had his own casino going at the back of the plane, complete with a green visor he'd brought with him and a little stick to push the £1-a-time bets around. It wasn't just for the players – lots of ordinary punters on the flight joined in for a quick bet and the stewardesses kept coming down with drinks. Talk about in-flight entertainment! Theo Foley came back at one stage to see how we were doing, just shook his head and went back.

Eventually, we got to our first refuelling stop, Abu Dhabi. You didn't have to get off the plane – you could stay on board if you wanted to. The Forest lads were ordered off but then I found a seat at the front of the plane with room for me to stretch out. I couldn't be bothered to get off and by then I fancied a little bit of a kip. I'd just got comfortable when I felt a tap on my legs and someone said, 'Young man!'

'Piss off,' I said, eyes closed.

'Young man, I won't ask you again.' It was Brian Clough, the Forest manager, and by the looks of him he'd been at the hospitality bar himself. Still, it *was* Cloughie, and you don't argue with a legend, sober or pissed. 'I'm telling you now, get off the plane and stretch your legs – it will do you good.'

It was like Kevin and Perry in the *Harry Enfield Show* where they're all meek and mild and say, 'Yes, Mrs Patterson,' when asked to do something. I immediately got up and left the plane, and looked around to see Paul Merson following me – Cloughie had found him too. Mind you, with all the publicity since about how good it is to keep moving around on long-haul flights to avoid deep vein thrombosis, Cloughie was years ahead of his time.

When we eventually landed at Brisbane, we all trooped through customs and immigration and got ready to board the coach to take us to the hotel. Then this big fuck-off limo about 20ft long pulled up. We all thought Rolf Harris or someone important was going to get out. Then its driver said, 'Has anyone seen Mr Clough?'

We were pissing ourselves as George looked around to see where his limo was. 'Theo!' he shouted. 'Theo, where's our car?' He obviously reckoned that if Brian Clough deserved a limo then he should have one too.

Me and Merse said, 'Don't worry, Gaffer – they're like buses, you wait ages then two will turn up at once.' But nothing did turn up and George had to get on the coach with the rest of us.

When the tournament began, our first game was against Queensland, the home side. George just said to us, 'Get this out of the way and then we're on our way to Great Keppel Island.'

Unfortunately, we lost 1–0. They were almost like Aussie-rule players, slapping us into the boards whenever they could. It was pandemonium as we lost in front of the 2,000 crowd and we couldn't wait to get off. George never lost it, but he wasn't happy. 'This is fucking embarrassing,' he said back in the dressing room, 'letting that bunch of Aussies beat us.'

Most of the teams were rotating their sides for the ten minutes each way game, but George kept the same side for the next game and gave us detailed instructions on how we should play. After it got under way, I could tell he wanted to hook me off but I was pretending that I couldn't hear him. He was moaning to the other lads on the bench, 'I know he can hear me.'

Afterwards, and we'd won, he said, 'That's much better.' Then turned to me and said, 'Grovesy, I wanted you off.'

I said, 'Sorry Gaffer, I couldn't hear you.'

He just looked at me and said, 'Oh yeah?'

We ended up finishing third in the tournament, and then we had a few days' break on the Gold Coast. We were taken to Great Keppel Island by boat and, as we set out, all the other lads from the other English sides were wearing shorts and flip-flops. It was about 100°F by then but still we had to get on the boat wearing our club blazers and ties. All the other teams were laughing their socks off as we sweltered in the heat and humidity, so I said to Tony Adams, 'Rodders, do us a favour and have a word with the Gaffer.'

So Rodders plucked up the courage and said, 'Any chance we can get changed, Boss?'

George just looked at him and said, 'No, Tony – we are the Arsenal. But I can see the lads are in trouble – tell them they can loosen their top buttons.' Later on, as we came down the gangplank, he said we could now take our blazers off. All heart, that man.

We were on Keppel Island for three or four days. It was like a holiday camp – a very upmarket holiday camp, but still a holiday camp. We would just take cans of Fosters down to the beach and have a drink. There wasn't all that much else to do, until I found out that we were just one and a half hours from the Great Barrier Reef by boat, and I suggested to the other lads we should go and see it.

'Fuck off, Grovesy,' they said. 'Who do you think you are? David Attenborough?'

But I told them that we might never get the chance again and eventually talked seven or eight of them into it. So off we went, taking snorkelling gear and everything for a swim when we got there. I was up for it – it sounded like a good day out.

The trouble was that as soon as the boat set out to sea I started to feel sick, and, of course, I was the only one. The others felt great. By the time we arrived, I was feeling terrible. All the other lads were on deck, having a swim and enjoying themselves and I was still down below thinking, I'm going to die. I hadn't been able to move.

Then one of the crew came down and said to me, 'What you want to do, mate, is to get in the water and you'll feel great.'

'What you want to do, mate,' I said, 'is fuck off.'

Eventually, we got back and after ten steps on dry land I felt fine. But the trip was one of the worst ideas I've had in my life, and that's saying something.

To fill in time during the break we asked the Gaffer if we could use the jet-skis but he said, 'No. I'm worried about injuries and I can't trust you lot.'

That was fair enough, but the Four Tops – David Rocastle, Gus Caesar, Mickey Thomas and Paul Davis – decided to go anyway. Obviously, they hoped the Boss wouldn't find out. As they got ready to head out to sea, Theo Foley was on the beach saying, 'I can't see you, it's nothing to do with me...'

So the lads headed out and then decided to play 'chicken' with each other. Theo was standing there saying 'Oh, for fuck's sake!'

Obviously, in 'chicken', you head straight for each other and wait until the last moment to see who loses their nerve and swerves away. Unfortunately, the lads hadn't thought it through. At the last minute, Gus and Rocky both decided to pull out and Gus turned to his left and Rocky veered to his right. Theo nearly fainted.

I won't go into detail, but after they smashed into each other they had to send another jet-ski out to bring Rocky back. He ended up being carried on to the beach and having his ankle strapped. At least it was the close season and he had to time to recover. Even so, I don't think the Gaffer was too pleased.

13

The Littlewoods Cup defeat at Wembley had been a real downer, but now the Boss was bringing in new players. The George Graham team was beginning to take shape.

Graham Rix had moved to Caen in France and in the summer of 1988 Steve Williams went to Luton. Kenny Sansom also departed for Newcastle. In came Brian Marwood from Sheffield Wednesday and as he played wide I thought the writing was on the wall for me. It meant there would be seven 'forward' players in the squad and that meant a lot of competition for places.

But the Gaffer had also been getting defenders in. He already had Tony Adams, who'd made his first-team debut in 1983 aged 17, and in May 1987 he'd signed Nigel Winterburn from Wimbledon. Nigel began playing right-back but now moved across to replace Kenny Sansom. In January 1988, he'd signed Lee Dixon from Stoke, and now he went back to the same club for

Steve Bould. Whether he knew it or not, the Gaffer had created a legend – the Arsenal back four was born.

They all got England caps, and they became famous in their own right. They're even mentioned in the hit film *The Full Monty* as a role model of how a group of men should move in unison. Three of them – Adams, Dixon and Winterburn – appear in the top ten of most appearances ever for Arsenal. Bouldie, who was born in Stoke and looked as though he'd been working down the pits since he was six, might have joined them but for the fact he was already in his mid-twenties when he signed. Take into account the fact that the man behind them for many years, David Seaman, is also in that top ten list, and you can see what I mean about George not wanting to change the team once he'd found players he was happy with.

There has not been a better back four anywhere in my opinion. As I said, they were all capped for England at some time or other, but I would have picked them all in one go. But I'll let you into a secret – I could have played in the Arsenal back four. Any of the other midfield players could have too. We did so much work against them in training we knew exactly how they operated.

Viv Anderson and Kenny Sansom – the full-backs George had inherited when he arrived – had both moved on and he would work for hours with the new ones, Lee and Nigel, to get them to show the opposition inside. Then the first centre-half would 'show' them to the next centre-half to shuffle the attackers across the pitch. The midfield were told to do the same as well, all aimed at making the opposition go sideways not forward.

George's big thing was 'cutting the line off'. He didn't want to see other teams getting down the line so they could put crosses in. If you were beaten during a game by a ball passed outside you, he would go mad.

He also made sure that our full-backs never fell behind the two centre-halves – the full-backs had to take their position from the centre-backs. That meant that when we didn't have the ball, when the back four were facing it, every one of the four always knew where the other three would be. George made sure it worked that way throughout the club: youth team, reserves, first team – they all had to know the routine. Other teams tried to do it, but they didn't put in the hours that George made sure we did. I think at times the guys would get bored, but it helped make them famous.

The four were also known for raising their arms for offside appeals with perfect timing, as if they were one man. George told them time and again, 'The linesman is your best friend.' When he got it right and raised his flag, the guys were told to say, 'Well done, lino.' But if the linesman – this was before they became 'referee's assistants'– got it wrong, they were told not to have a go at him, because it would cause him to take revenge later in the game by letting the opposition get away with a close call.

The best way to beat the flat back four, I thought, was to play a deep-lying centre-forward, a bit like Nigel Clough played at times for Nottingham Forest, and then releasing the ball to the runners, the guys making a break through the line. It sounds easy in theory, but in practice it was really hard to do.

We also worked for hours on other aspects of the game too, not just the defending. If we were attacking wide but couldn't get to the by-line, the Gaffer told us always to cross it to the near post. If we did get to the by-line, though, then always float it to the back post. That meant that the other guys in the team had a pretty good idea what the man with the ball was going to do with it.

We worked on set-pieces all the time too. For corners, we had near-post flick-ons and we scored many goals in matches that way. It was because everyone knew what was going to happen, what position we should be in and what runs we should be making. When anything like that worked on a Saturday, it was because we had worked so hard on it during the week.

George was often accused of turning out robots with the system that he played, but you needed to have intelligence to make it work. All his instructions were simple and straightforward, though – they had to be, because even I understood them.

So, things were starting to look good at the back, but they weren't looking so good for me. I was out of the picture: I couldn't get in the starting line-up and Martin Hayes was often chosen as the sub.

Sometimes I used the football agent Eric 'Monster' Hall to arrange things for me. Eric knew nothing about football, but he realised early on that there was money to be made out of players. He arranged a boot deal with Puma for me – I think I got £1,000 and Eric got half of it. I could have all the Puma gear I wanted for the year too. Or he might arrange for me to open a restaurant or something and I'd get £300 for my troubles. He was never my agent really, though, because I never had one. I don't like them. I don't think they're any good for the game.

Eric used to look at the football reports to see which of his clients were playing and which ones weren't. So, if you were out of the side, he'd be in touch with you pretty soon. I'd been injured and then dropped, so Eric called me one day and said, 'Go and put a transfer request in.' I wasn't having that, so he came up with another idea that might get me away. 'Start a fight in training,' he told me. 'If you start a fight, the club won't want you.'

'Are you fucking mad?' I said. 'I don't want to start trouble. He's buried internationals and I would be lucky to make the reserves for the next two years!'

In the meantime, Arsenal were doing well away at the start of the season but struggling at home, and in September we were trailing to Southampton 2–1 at Highbury. We managed to get a 2–2 result, but there had been some needle during the game and that night it was big news that Paul Davis had broken the jaw of Glenn Cockerill, the Southampton player. Davo was very unlucky. He had obviously waited and waited until there was a corner and everyone's eyes would be elsewhere, and then he larruped him. It was totally out of character for Davo – he wasn't that sort of player, so obviously something had wound him up.

The problem was the punch was just caught in the corner of the camera shot. Another half-inch and no one would have known about it – apart from Glenn Cockerill, that is. He couldn't manage solids for two weeks and Davo got a nine-match ban and a £3,000 fine for bringing the game into disrepute. As I've said, getting back in the Arsenal side once you were out was very hard and, even when his suspension was over, he only managed a few more games that season.

While we're on the subject, we weren't a dirty team at all. Bouldie and Rodders could look after themselves and David Rocastle was a lot tougher than people realised. All the lads could mix it if need be and Wimbledon and their Crazy Gang – the so-called hard men of the day – never bullied us. The Boss would sometimes tell us to 'steam into them' when talking about opponents, or he'd say 'test him' if he wanted someone tried out for courage, but he never went further than that.

In October, I managed to get back in the side and played up front alongside Smudge at Upton Park against West Ham. We won 4–1 so I was in the starting line-up against Manchester United for the Mercantile Credit Centenary Trophy at Villa Park.

The trophy was to celebrate 100 years of the Football League and was one of those tournaments that helped fill the European-ban gap. There was no such thing as a 'small game' for a club like Arsenal, especially not against Manchester United, and there were about 35,000 in the ground. It was one of Davo's last games before his ban began and he scored one goal and made another. I remember Brian McClair was on fire for United and they had guys like Bryan Robson and Mark Hughes in their side.

So we were in a good mood as we climbed up the stairs to the Villa Park directors' box to get our trophy. I noticed a gorgeous bird near by who was watching us and said to Merse in front of me, 'Look at that blonde!' Then I turned round to Steve Bould, who was behind me, and said, 'Hey, she's got half a chance, Bouldie – she wants a ginga.'

As we walked past her, she said, 'Well done, boys,' and then looked at me and said, 'Well done, Perry.'

'Fucking hell,' I muttered to Bouldie. 'She can have a bit of ginger if she wants it.'

But then, as Bouldie reached her, she threw her arms around him and said, 'I'm so proud of my little brother.'

Oh dear! Bouldie wasn't the sort you'd want to upset, but he took it as a joke. He'd invited his family down from Stoke for the game and we met up with her in the bar afterwards, though just to be on the safe side I kept saying, 'Bouldie, J is for joke.'

14

There's a lot of bollocks talked about footballers and drink. You might have read in the past about players regularly going out for big matches still hungover from the night before. Sure, there were a couple of incidents at Arsenal that I can recall when a player was the worse for wear, and once, by accident, I ended up playing when I wasn't, shall we say, 100 per cent, but that was because I hadn't expected to play.

There were just a very small handful of incidents over a number of years, and to think that you could go out boozed-up and play football at the highest level on a regular basis is just stupid. We didn't do that at Arsenal – we'd got our drinking too well organised for that! As well as being one of the best sides in the country at playing football, we also had the Tuesday Club, so called because Tuesday was the day we let our hair down.

It makes sense when you think about it. Fridays were out of the question because you would normally be playing on a

Saturday. A lot of people think that Saturdays is when footballers go wild, but that's when they go out with their wives and girlfriends, not when they go out with the lads. In my case, I wouldn't hang around in London anyway. When I was playing at Arsenal, I'd go back to Colchester to unwind. But there was always Tuesday...

Unless we had a match on the Wednesday – in which case the Tuesday Club would have to postpone its activities – this was the perfect day for us. We didn't go to the training ground at London Colney on Tuesdays – we would go to Highbury itself, so we were virtually in the middle of London. Most of the guys would park their cars at the JVC centre at around 9.45am, ready for the 10am start. That meant that the motors would be safe or, if they didn't make it back, they'd be handy for them to pick up the next day. I always made sure I came in on the train – I knew I wouldn't be in any condition to drive home. We'd get through 15 to 20 pints or bottles of lager each on an average Tuesday – if it was quiet!

It was mainly running during those Tuesday mornings at the ground, either round the track or up and down the terraces. George would say, 'This is how we used to do it in the 1970s,' and we'd say the usual, 'No wonder you look so good, Gaffer,' and all that stuff. We were taking the piss out of him but he was probably fitter than when he used to play.

Normally, for training you'd arrive in a tracksuit or something casual. Tuesdays were different and we'd turn up in shirts and nice trousers – pulling gear, in other words. We'd have bags, shaving gear, hair gel, the works. Normally, it was me, Rodders, Bouldie, Merse, Nigel Winterburn and Kevin Richardson. That was the core of the Club, although others would join in from time to time. Later, Andy Linighan, Colin Pates and Jimmy Carter became members.

We'd do our training that morning and then get ready for the real hard work. George would come in and he obviously knew what we were up to, because he would ask, 'Where is it later then?'

'Later' would often start at the Alwyn Castle pub, just down the road from the ground and near Highbury Corner. It was handy for a first stop and, although there would be a few fans who might come up for a chat, no one really bothered us. Some of the girls from the offices at the ground – Sue, Karen and Lyn – would come in and it would all be very civilised.

They'd have to go back at the end of lunchtime so then we had a big decision to make: where to move on to next. Rodders knew one bar by King's Cross or there was another one down the Holloway Road. It was always pints of lager – no sophisticated wine nonsense.

When it got to nighttime, we would go to the Punch and Judy pub in Covent Garden, or perhaps TGI Fridays. It would be 8 or 9pm by then and we probably hadn't eaten, but food was not a priority! By this stage, there would be a couple of birds in tow. The lads were always on the pull and there would be different girls coming and going. They weren't groupies as such – they just seemed to be there.

There was one girl we called the Queen of the Groupies – though not to her face – who always seemed to find us. She was a super girl – blonde, skinny, long legs and she always brought a couple of darlings with her. She'd started out a while earlier as the mistress of one of the married internationals at the club, and when that ended she just stayed hanging around. I guess at one stage she was having different players – but never me!

Later on, when I finished my career playing a few games for Dagenham and Redbridge, there she was again. She'd started at the Gunners and worked her way down. She was engaged to one of the younger players there and he was really in love with her.

If I'd had too much to drink, which was every Tuesday, my wife Mandy knew that I'd be on the last train from Liverpool Street to Colchester just after midnight. But there were two problems: one was I rarely got there in time for the train, and, two, if I did get there in time, I couldn't see the departure board, I was in such bad shape.

Once, I did make it in time but I couldn't read the board to find out which platform my train was on. So I asked this young lad holding a football to tell me when my train was leaving. As I was asking him, I borrowed his ball, saying, 'I'm Perry Groves – I play for Arsenal.' I kept it in the air twice but then it went on the line.

'You must be Perry Groves then,' he said, as it bounced along the track.

If I did catch the train, there was always the problem of making sure I got off at the right station. I once woke up at Stowmarket at 1.30am and by then, of course, I'd sobered up. I was in the middle of nowhere and it was freezing cold, but I managed to find a mini-cab firm open. The problem was I had no money. The driver said to me, in his thick Stowmarket accent, 'You be going where?'

He wouldn't take me back to Colchester as I had no cash, but I told him my dad was living in Stowmarket at the time and he agreed to take me there. He asked me who my dad was and I said, 'Ginger Groves,' and he said, 'Oh, I know Ginger.'

It was snowing by this time so when we got to Dad's place I started to throw snowballs at his window to wake him up. He opened the window, looked at me and just said, 'London, train, pissed.'

I said, 'Right. Lend me 30 spots, will you?'

When I eventually got home, I climbed into bed and said to Mandy, 'You will never...' but she just said, 'I don't want to know.'

Occasionally, the Tuesday Club would have an outing, and one day Rodders organised one to Towcester Races for his birthday. He'd arranged for a minibus to pick us up at the training ground at London Colney at about 10.30am. When it arrived, we stacked it with crates of lager and off we went.

By the time we got there, we were well away and we decided to club our money. Word soon got around there was a syndicate at the course placing bets. The trouble was, we were the world's worst gamblers – we had not got a Scooby. Every bet we had was either on a clothes horse, a rocking horse or a sea horse. We didn't win a dinar.

As we headed down the motorway, we asked Rodders where we were going. He said there was a launch party for the *Daily Sport* at Stringfellows and he had been invited. Now one of Rodders's nicknames was Billy Liar because he was always making things up, so we thought, Here we go again. We parked outside Stringfellows and there were all these birds going in with their Charlies hanging out. As we got out, we still reckoned it was just a wind-up and we'd be just going to the pub next door, but then we saw Rodders going in the club, so we followed.

We went in and the place was heaving, but the doormen said to us, 'No, gentlemen – you are downstairs.' So down we went and found there was a roped-off area with a notice saying 'Arsenal VIP'. Well done, Rodders.

Soon we were saying, 'Bring all the birds on,' and then the Queen of the Groupies arrived with five other girls. She always used to have lots of girls who did 'promotion' work hanging around, and one of them was a tall blonde who looked a bit like Kim Basinger. At least she did through my mince-pies, given the state I was in. I remember – smooth bastard that I am – putting a rose in my mouth and saying to her, 'Go on, take it.' I know we all ended up somewhere together, the players and this group of birds, but I can't remember much about what happened – I was so pissed.

I can remember when Jimmy Carter first joined the Tuesday Club, though. He'd just been signed from Liverpool for £500,000 and I said to him, 'Do you like a sherbet?' and he said yes. So we took him to AJ's at Apex Corner, one of our regular places. We'd only had four or five pints of lager – nothing for us – when he started taking the piss out of everybody. I thought, This bloke is settling quicker than snow. Then I felt my right leg getting warm so I looked down – he'd pissed on it. I was furious – they were my best strides.

So I went to the khazi to get myself dry and Jimmy – 'Peanut' we called him, after the American President who'd been a peanut farmer – came in. As I was mopping myself, I felt my other trouser leg get warm – he'd pissed on that too. Then Merse came in and Peanut pissed on his trousers as well. We wanted to rip his head off, but everyone was laughing their heads off. 'I'm sorry,' Peanut said, 'I can't drink.' Come 5.45pm, there was Jimmy collapsed in a heap. Crikey, I thought, we're not that bad, are we?

On Thursday at training, Jimmy was as quiet as a mouse, and he gave us money to buy new strides. Merse had told him, 'You are banned – you're not coming out with the Tuesday Club again!' but he was such a lovely guy we changed our minds.

15

I thought you might like to know a little bit about the 'bonding' that takes place at football clubs. Part of this is done at pre-season or mid-season breaks. They're usually in hot countries – Spain is a favourite – but they always involve drink.

My first experience of this was at Colchester United at the end of the 1984–85 season when we went to Magaluf in Majorca and spent a week in a hotel. All season we had been putting the money from our fines into a kitty. We thought we'd be in with all the birds, but then Everton arrived and pissed on our bonfire. They had players like Andy Gray and Pat van den Hauwe on about £1,000 a week and stayed in a luxury five-star hotel while we were in the Bates Motel. It was hard with Everton's stars around – but I still managed to get lucky.

It was also the first time I got into the drink culture. I wasn't the biggest drinker in the world, so I'd have three or four bottles during the day and that would be enough for me. I'd already be incoherent as everyone was getting ready to go out, and I missed the first two nights as I couldn't make it. I even got prickly heat too!

Our manager Cyril Lea gave us a speech on the coach from the airport saying, 'You are representing England. If anyone gets in trouble with fighting or loutish behaviour he will be on the first plane home and fined two weeks' wages.' We said, 'Yes, Gaffer.' That night we passed a bar and there was a ruckus going on – it was Cyril grappling with a local. We shouted, 'Go on, Gaffer.' He just said, 'I was provoked.'

Arsenal's trips were much better – it was like the Tuesday Club by the seaside. In my early days there, we went on a summer jolly-up to Cyprus at the end of the 1986–87 season. Kevin Keegan and George Best were also on the island playing for an invitation team. Graham Rix knew Keegan from their England days so he said, 'Come on, chaps – we're going to see KK.'

So off we all went to a restaurant and there were Keegan and Best at a table having a meal. I was introduced to Keegan and when I said hello to George, he replied, 'Hello, son.' I went to the bar as Rixie carried on talking to them. Then the restaurant owner came over to the table and asked if he could bring someone over to meet George, and George said yes. Then I saw this blonde vision of beauty, the most glorious woman I had ever seen, come over and the manager introduced her.

George looked at her briefly and said hello, but then blanked her. I couldn't believe it. This was the most gorgeous woman I had ever seen and it looked as though he didn't want to know her. Kevin stood up and said hello to her properly and was polite, but George just looked at his plate and carried on eating.

Then, all of a sudden, he looked her straight in the eyes and said, 'Are we fucking later?' She giggled and then, after a moment, said, 'All right.' George just said, 'We'll catch up with each other later,' and carried on eating. She went off, happy as could be, and I realised I had just seen a master operator in action. Smooth bastard. What she did to George that night I've no idea, but I know he had to pull out of his game and fly home the next day!

It was on that trip that I bumped into Steve Foster, the centre-half who'd welcomed me to the big boys' world by clattering me when I played against him at Luton. We'd hired a minibus to go to Aya Napa as we'd heard it was full of Swedish birds, and about seven or eight of us went over there. We'd been in a bar for a while and decided to walk down towards the beach when we saw this big bloke with a perm heading towards us. It was Steve Foster, followed by the Luton team. They were on a break too and before long we were all in a bar playing darts. A £1 Cyprus note was pinned on the board and the game was to hit it. Fossie said to me, 'Me and you, one dart each, £50. If you hit it I give you £50 and vice versa.'

I told him that if we played for money it would end up as a row, but I'd play him if we could hit the other guy over the head with our flip-flops if we hit the note. 'I like that,' he said. 'That's a good game.' What he didn't know was that I'd got leather heels on my sandals while his were just lightweight plastic.

He could hardly hit the wall, let alone the £1 note and after the third time he'd lost and I'd taken a run-up and smashed my flip-flops over his head, I said to him, 'You're playing with the big boys now.'

Now one of the Luton players was Mick Harford, their centre-forward who hardly ever said anything and had an intimidating look about him – I'll tell you another story about him later. Anyway, as I was walking away I felt a hand on my shoulder and

I turned round. He was looking me straight in the eye and he said, deadpan, 'That is really funny', and walked off.

Another trip with the Gooners was a mid-season one to Marbella for four or five days. It was training in the morning, and then some 'bonding'. Merse and I broke away one afternoon and went to the harbour. We went into a bar at the furthest side of the harbour and decided to have half a beer there and the same in every bar to work our way round the bay.

In the second bar there was a busker playing 'American Pie', which was Merse's favourite song, so we decided to take him with us everywhere we went. What we didn't know was that 'American Pie' was the only song he knew, so by the time we got to the 15th bar we were getting a bit fed up with it, so we gave him the slip.

Then we found our way to a water park. It was closed as it was February, so we climbed over the fence. I had the idea to run up the circular tube-slide to the top and come down the steps on the other side. The only problem was, when I got to the top I found they'd taken the steps away for the winter. Then the manager came out and started shouting at me, so the only way out for me was to come back down the slide on my hands and knees and get out quick. He wasn't happy. Merse, of course, had done a runner when he realised what was happening. I caught up with him back at Puerto Banus and we ended up squirting ketchup over each other just to round off the evening.

There's a saying in the film world that affairs on location don't count. Well, it's the same in football. We say, 'When you fly over the water, it doesn't count.' Our own code of silence is, 'What goes on on tour stays on tour.' Bloody good job.

On one of our Spanish trips, we were staying at the Andalusia Plaza Hotel on the Costa del Sol and a couple of the lads went into Puerto Banus. For once, I didn't go with them and I was in my room late that night when there was a knock on the door. I opened it and there were two of the lads – both internationals and household names – with a blonde the like of whom you only see in a dream. Talk about gorgeous! This was sex on legs – and more. Tall, blonde and beautiful, she was English too, so we could talk to her – not that talking was on the agenda. One of the lads said they'd been to the casino playing blackjack and, turning to me, said, 'Look what I won.'

It didn't take long before all three of them were at it with me watching – all right, I joined in for a bit of a play, but not the real thing. Anyway, just as everything was reaching its climax – in every sense of the word – the blonde turned to one of the lads and said, 'You live my way, don't you?'

The blood drained from his face – and everywhere else too. She explained she lived near him in north London and had seen him out and about. Obviously, she flew over to Spain for, shall we say, a working holiday every now and then. So here was proof that it really is a small world, and suddenly my mate realised this little bit of nonsense wouldn't necessarily stay on tour and could come back to haunt him. The thought of bumping into his new lady friend at Brent Cross shopping centre or wherever, and having to explain it all, meant he lost his appetite for the moment, so to speak.

It didn't bother our other pal, though – he kept on, no problem. Perhaps he didn't shop at Brent Cross.

16

In the autumn of 1988, we got drawn away to Liverpool in the Littlewoods Cup. They were still the side to beat, but we went up there and hammered them, though all we got to show for it was a 1–1 draw. We should have won by four goals but we came away thinking, Hey, we're not bad. There were no goals down at our place, with 54,000 watching and an estimated 5,000 locked out, and they eventually won the play-off 2–1 after more than five hours of football.

I got injured around this time, so I was with some mates in a pub in Colchester watching our game against Nottingham Forest and there were a couple of 'chip' local players in there. I call them 'chip' because they have chips on their shoulders because they never made it. We went 1–0 down and they went, 'Fucking useless Arsenal,' but we ended up winning 4–1. At the end of the game, one of them came over and started to give me some more stick, so I said, 'Look, do me a favour and fuck off. You're a would-have, could-have, should-have.'

'What makes you better than me?' he insisted.

Now, if you're injured, you still get win bonuses for a while, so I pointed to the screen and replied, 'I just got £350 for that, that's what.'

For some reason, people think they can go up to footballers and start slaughtering them. The reason that they haven't made it – unless they've had a bad injury – is that they weren't good enough. You have to have determination, desire, bottle, character – call it what you will. Pure ability and talent is not enough: you need something else – we call it 'arsehole'.

I am not saying I was good enough to play for England, and I would never say I should have played for England, but I had more ability than some England internationals and some lower-division players had more ability than I did. Around the time I was playing, Carlton Palmer and Geoff Thomas played for England and they got a lot of stick from people who said they weren't good enough. But I would never go up to these guys and say, 'You didn't deserve to play for England.' Where you end up playing is where you deserve to be.

Boxing Day 1988 turned out to be hotter in London than it was on the Costa del Sol. We were away at Charlton that day and won 3–2 to go top of the First Division, but that was only part of the story.

As it was a Boxing Day match, we would meet up and do a little bit of light training the previous evening – Christmas Day. Before the match, the Boss had told us, 'I'm trusting you – no drinking' and we all turned up for at Highbury for our 5pm meeting. All of us, that is, except for two players. We were all saying they'd be fined when Nigel burst in the room and told us that one of them was 'pissed – paralytic!'

This player had his family down for the holidays, but he was also in dispute with the Boss at the time – he seemed to have forgotten that the Gaffer had rescued him. So, when he walked in, he looked as though he had got myxomatosis: he was bleary-eyed, his breath smelled of booze – and he was wearing carpet slippers. We started to say, 'If the Gaffer comes in...' but all he said was, 'Fucking Jock bastard.'

So there we were in our Arsenal tracksuits and there he was in his slippers. A couple of the senior players said, 'You're pissed. Get through training, have a shower, get on the coach and go to the hotel.'

You could smell him at training – it was like a brewery. His co-ordination had gone and he was practically falling over. At one stage, he went for a shot by the near post and the ball almost hit the Clock. All the crosses were aimed at him and every time the ball hit his head we all winced.

After a while, George said, 'That's it, we're finished' and we all came off the pitch to go to the Noke Hotel at St Albans, where we were to stay the night.

The player managed to get his Arsenal tracksuit on, but he was still wearing slippers as we put him near the back of the coach. George said nothing and the player was muttering, 'Why can't you have a drink at Christmas? Tight Scotch twat...' and stuff like that.

The next day he was in the team when we beat Charlton (although we didn't deserve to) but he wasn't in the swing of things. Their midfield player Steve MacKenzie, who looked as though he'd had a couple of big Christmas dinners himself, still managed to score twice and our rather merry player didn't pick him up for either of them.

After a game like that, where the performance wasn't great but the result was, George would normally say something like,

'Crap performance, good win.' This time was different. He let rip at this player. 'You're a fucking disgrace. They've got you out of trouble,' he went on, meaning the rest of the side. 'I can't believe you let MacKenzie get away like that. You've let everybody down – your teammates, your family, everyone.'

We were all sitting there saying nothing as George stormed out.

The player started to take his boots off but then said, 'You fucking bastards! Which one of you told him?'

We all burst out laughing. No one had told George – no one needed to. 'You couldn't run, you couldn't stand and you were wearing carpet slippers!' I said to him. 'You work it out.' He wouldn't have it though – he was convinced someone had bubbled him.

Over the New Year, I came on as sub when we played at Aston Villa and scored, so I was in the starting line-up for the home league game with West Ham, who had knocked us out of the FA Cup after a replay. It was a scrappy game and I was having, shall we say, an indifferent period when I put us into the lead after 56 minutes. I rose like a salmon at the far post and headed the ball back across the goal. But I got a far better header on it than I meant to and it looped towards the far corner of the net.

Just as their centre-half Gary Strodder jumped to head it away, someone shot him. Only joking – it just looked as though he'd been shot. What really happened was that the ground slopes down by the goal line and he hadn't realised it as he launched himself upwards. He got it all wrong, came down too soon and the ball sailed into the net. We ended up winning 2–1 and as we came off I remember thinking, That's got me out of jail, and I might keep my place.

'Well done, chaps,' said the Boss. 'Poor performance, good result.

Training on Monday and Tuesday, Wednesday off, back in Thursday.' We all thought, Great, but then he added, 'Everybody apart from you, Grovesy. You're playing for the reserves on Tuesday.'

It meant I was dropped. Those were the hard games to play in. If three or four of the squad were playing, then it was all right, but if it was just you... All the other guys would say things like, 'It's just to get you fit,' but they knew just as well as you did what the score was. I knew I'd been bombed.

By February, we were still very much in the hunt for the Championship when we had to play Millwall at The Den, their old ground. That was nice, I can tell you. They had players like Teddy Sheringham and Tony Cascarino in their side, but they were the least of our troubles. There were only about 14,000–15,000 there, but we all know about their fans.

I was sub and as soon as their supporters saw me they started chanting, 'Rent boy, rent boy – hang 'im, hang 'im, hang 'im.' I was quite moved, I can tell you. I did a few stretches and bent over in front of them, so that got them going even more. George told me I had to warm up in front of them every 15 minutes or so just to keep warm. Thanks a lot.

The game ended 0–0, but the most exciting part came when Tony Adams thought he had scored. The ball was about a yard over the line when their goalkeeper clawed it away, so he was right to be upset when the referee David Elleray said it wasn't a goal. Rodders chased him back to the halfway line screaming at him and he was eventually booked for dissent.

Now Rodders was the Boss's blue-eyed boy but he said to him afterwards, 'It's not becoming of an Arsenal captain. The directors are on to me that it's not the behaviour we expect from our captain.'

Rodders maintained his innocence and insisted that he hadn't abused him. Unfortunately, what he didn't know was that the Football League were carrying out an experiment and Elleray had been wired up during the game. Everything that he said or was said close to him was picked up by the mike. How's your luck, eh?

It turned out that Rodders had screamed at him – in a high-pitched, Aled Jones voice – 'You fucking cheat, you fucking cheat, you fucking cheat!' Then he started shouting, 'It's my goal, it's my goal, it's my goal!' Then he finished off with: 'You cheating, fucking bastard!'

Eventually. Elleray managed to get a word in and said, 'Calm down, Tony.'

'Sorry. David,' Rodders said, 'I just get so excited.' He still got booked though.

I hadn't been in the starting line-up all that much, but at the end of February 1989 the Boss made Paul Merson sub and I started against Luton Town, the team who had beaten us at Wembley almost a year earlier. There was no score for over an hour until Steve Bould headed a corner on towards me. I was on the edge of the six-yard box and chested the ball, then suddenly I came up with an overhead kick and the ball was in the corner of the net. The crowd went mad – perhaps it was a massive sigh of relief as we hadn't won for a while. It was one of the best goals I ever scored.

We got a second in the 90th minute through Smudge Smith – his first goal for a while. I was pleased for him, but annoyed too because I would have had the headlines all to myself if he hadn't scored.

The reporters were all waiting for me when I came out of the dressing room, but it wasn't my goal they wanted to talk about. During the game, I'd been off towards their goal when someone fouled me from behind. I turned round to square up to whoever did it, only to see Mick Harford, their centre-forward. He looked like a cross between Jack Palance and Norman 'Psycho' Bates, so as I went for him I was thinking, Fucking hell, I hope someone comes and separates us quick!

Rodders and Alan Smith grabbed hold of me, thank God, so I knew I was safe. Once I was sure they'd got a firm grip on me, I started saying things like, 'I'm going to kill him!' even though my hands were safe behind my back and someone had got hold of Harford too. And then he went and spat in my face. This slow-motion gob came across and landed all over me – it was disgusting.

As soon as they let go of me, I went for him, and I wasn't pretending this time. I was so angry I lost it. There was a big kerfuffle but it was all finished quickly and no one even got booked. He was out of order but he was too big, too mean and too hard for me to go for him in the tunnel!

Three things are out of order in football: over-the-top tackles, elbows in the face and spitting. I think spitting is the worst of the lot and if someone spits on you then you should be allowed to punch them in the face. So, when I came out of the changing rooms into the marble halls at Highbury, all the reporters were waiting to talk to me. But it wasn't about my wonder goal.

'What have you got to say about Harford spitting at you?' they said. 'We all saw it.'

I just smiled and said, 'He didn't spit at me.'

'So why wipe it away then?' they asked.

'I was just sweating profusely,' I said, adding with a grin, 'I sweat quite a lot, being a finely tuned athlete.'

But they knew and I knew.

A few minutes later, I had to go back to the changing room for something and the 'away' dressing room was next to ours. This big wooden door opens and Harford walks through it. There was no one else in sight, just him and me. Oh shit. He had one of those 'I'm going to kill you' faces anyway and he called out, 'Oi, you!' I said, 'Yeah?' and we faced each other like a showdown in a Spaghetti Western. Seconds seem like minutes, all that stuff. Then he just said, 'Thanks,' and turned and walked away.

I took that as an apology – well, the nearest I was going to get to one – because if I had gone public he probably would have been charged with bringing the game into disrepute. But he couldn't say sorry – that would have ruined his hard-man image. I wouldn't say we ever became mates, but he did turn up some years later to my benefit golf day, so it looks as though he still thinks I'm all right.

17

The next month, March 1989, we played at Southampton. I remember it for quite a few reasons. One was that we wore one of the worst kits I ever went out in. We had yellow shirts and white shorts which made us look like a pub team (the worst kit was a sort of blue, yellow and white diamond pattern we had in the FA Cup at Wrexham, when we looked like court jesters).

Another reason I remember the game well was that I scored the first goal, we went on to win 3–1, and it kept up our push for the Championship. But the main reason it sticks in my mind is that during the first half the ball was in the air, I went up for it and their centre-half, Neil 'Razor' Ruddock, went for it too. I think he started his run from his own penalty area, but he caught me on the back of the head. There was blood coming out and I rubbed it, as I always did, to make it look worse. Gary Lewin came on to look at me and said I would have to have it stitched.

The Southampton doctor came to look at me and Gary told him

not to give me an anaesthetic as he thought there would be a reaction. But the doctor decided to do it anyway and gave me an injection in the scalp, just like a dentist does in your gums, and then gave me four stitches. In the dressing room at half-time, I felt groggy, as I'd never had an injection in my head before.

Then, five or ten minutes into the second half, I was by their far post and thinking, I don't feel well here, and then I puked up all over the line. I felt terrible, so Smudge called over to the bench and said, 'Get him off.' That was my first encounter with the medical team at Southampton. It wasn't to be the last.

At the end of February, we had 19 points ahead of Liverpool in the league, but we had a poor March and by the start of April, when we drew 1-1 at Manchester United, the gap had been reduced to just three points. That Old Trafford game was the start of Tony Adams being labelled a donkey by fans. He scored a great, brave, diving header but a few minutes later he sliced the ball over our own keeper John Lukic into the net. Those lovely, charming Mancs then started calling him a donkey and began making hee-haw sounds. I was upset – the quality of carrots they threw was very poor...

By 15 April, the title run-in was tighter than ever. We had a chance of putting more pressure on Liverpool because they were in an FA Cup semi-final against Nottingham Forest at Hillsborough, so they wouldn't be picking up any league points that day. We beat Newcastle at home 1-0 with a goal from Brian Marwood and the Boss had unleashed me in the 89th minute when I went on for David Rocastle. Still, it was three points in the bag and we all came off the pitch buzzing. As we were leaving the field, we could hear people saying that the Hillsborough semi-final had been abandoned, but we didn't have any idea why.

In the dressing room, George said, 'Well done,' and the rest of it, but by the time we had changed it was obvious something serious had happened. Pat Rice had a TV in the coaches' room and there were images of people being carried away on stretchers and a voice came over saying that there had been fatalities.

At the start, they were saying that 30 people had died, and all the euphoria of our win suddenly went out of the window. People were quiet and shaking their heads. We thought what we had just done was important, but it paled into insignificance now. I remember driving home and hearing the death toll was rising all the time. There was even talk of Liverpool not playing any more games that season.

In all 96 people died at the Liverpool fans' end at Hillsborough, crushed to death. It would change football in this country forever, as all-seater stadiums were subsequently introduced to prevent a similar tragedy happening again.

On the Monday, George spoke to all the players and said that, although there was tremendous sympathy for all the victims and their relatives, we had to carry on doing our jobs. That's exactly what we did, and, when we won 1–0 at Middlesbrough at the start of May, we were eight points clear at the top. But Liverpool had games in hand and we didn't do ourselves any favours a week later when we lost at home 2–1 to Derby County. I came on as sub for Merse and I was on the bench, as usual, a few days later when we played Wimbledon at home.

Both the Gunners and Liverpool now had just two league games left, so it was a game that we had to win to put pressure on Liverpool. Nigel Winterburn, for the first time in his life, hit a ball with his right foot and scored from 30 yards, but we ended up drawing 2–2. That meant we were top, but only because we had scored more goals, and the game Liverpool had in hand was at home to West Ham.

There was a crowd of 40,000 for the Wimbledon game, our final home game of the season, and when it was over we thanked the fans for their support that year. One report said, 'Arsenal last night bade farewell to their supporters and almost certainly to the First Division title.' It wasn't looking good.

But because of Hillsborough there was such a fixture backlog that for the first time the last game of the season would be played after the FA Cup Final. Liverpool were in that too and beat Everton 3–2 after extra-time, and so the last week of the season began.

Liverpool had two games to play, the first at home to West Ham United, the second against us, also at Anfield. Liverpool just had to beat West Ham at home and that was that really. The Hammers were famous for throwing the towel in away from home and you had more chance of finding rocking-horse shit than them getting a result up there. I listened to the game on the radio and when Liverpool won 5–1 I thought that was it. It meant that we didn't just have to win at Anfield – we had to beat them by two goals or more.

We went in for training the next day and we all thought the season was over. In fact, since the Wimbledon result, we'd been very relaxed and casual. We were all mentally wound down, but perhaps that was a good thing because if we'd spent the ten days after Wimbledon thinking about nothing but the Liverpool match we would have gone mental.

That May, the weather was fantastic. I would do some light training, winding down really, and I'd be home in my back garden by 1.30pm. The big drink then was a bottle of Sol with a slice of lime in it, and I would have five or six of those. It was like the close season.

During that time, I remember me, Merse, Rodders and Bouldie

saying that, if we could win at Liverpool, we would become legends. We were always seeing members of the 1971 Double team – the one George had played in – around Highbury, and we reckoned that it would shut them up. They were great players, of course, but it used to piss us off seeing them around all the time and hear people going on about that side.

After West Ham had rolled over and died, the Boss said to us, 'At least now we know what we have to do. We have to beat them by two clear goals.' He was taking a squad of 16 up there, and every professional on the club's books would be going, just to show the Arsenal team spirit.

The game was to be played on the Friday night – the first time incidentally that the title had been decided by the last game since 1899 – and on the Wednesday George spoke to us all at London Colney. 'Everyone thinks we are going to go gung-ho,' he said, 'but I've decided to play a sweeper.' David O'Leary was going to play behind Rodders and Bouldie, with Rocky, Richo and Michael Thomas in midfield. Smudge and Merse would be up front. We all looked at each other and thought he'd gone mad, but he said, 'If we concede an early goal we're fucked. What I want to do is go in at half time at 0–0, then I'll be happy.'

David O'Leary had played as a sweeper a couple of times recently, and George's big thing was that we weren't to concede a goal. All these so-called experts on television – Ron Atkinson, David Pleat and the rest – were all saying that we would be pushing the full-backs forward from the start. They were all talking through their arses. The Boss was saying that, if we could nick a goal in the first 10 or 15 minutes of the second half, then Liverpool would get jittery and in the last 15–20 minutes we could have a go. 'I tell you, chaps, I really fancy us,' he said.

I turned to our assistant manager Theo Foley a little later and said, 'Theo, has he really lost it? He's lost the plot. He'll start doing chicken impressions next,' and then the rest of the players all began doing chicken impressions.

'Don't you think we've got a chance?' Theo asked.

'We've got two,' I said. 'Slim and no.'

After all, we hadn't won at Anfield in 15 years, Liverpool had gone 24 games without being beaten, and they hadn't conceded two goals there to anyone since 1986! If they won the Championship, it would be their eighth triumph in ten years and the second Double in three years. But George still believed it was possible. All the pundits kept saying that we would be flying into them from the kick-off, we had to get an early goal and all that stuff, but that was totally the opposite of what George had planned.

We knew the Arsenal fans would wonder what we were doing playing three centre-backs, but George told all three of them – David O'Leary, Rodders and Bouldie – not to go anywhere. They had to be disciplined. George wasn't born with just one silver spoon for luck in his mouth. He must have been born with two – but he was a brilliant coach too.

We travelled up before 10am on Friday morning, which was early, but that was George's decision. Normally, the first-team coach would be half-full, but this time it was packed with players and directors and vice-presidents and the like. There were even directors there who I think they had to dig up – one was practically a corpse.

When I got on board there was an old man in my regular seat. 'Out!' I said, adding, 'These are our lucky seats, so sit there if you want us to get beat. If you move, we might win.' He moved.

We were all pretty jovial as we travelled up. It was almost like a day out as no one was expecting us to win. There were plenty of cars with Arsenal scarves as we drove up the motorway and lots of the fans gave us the thumbs-up.

When we got to the hotel in Liverpool, we had pasta for lunch as usual and then I shared a room with Merse – which was a pain in the arse as he was always on the phone in the room trying to put a bet on. We normally watched an episode of *Neighbours* and talked about which of the actresses in it we would like to shag and then I'd try and have a kip some time between 2pm and 5pm. A lot of players take sleeping tablets at night before a match, but not for a daytime sleep.

We had a 5pm wake-up call and then went downstairs in our club blazers and ties for some tea and toast. Then George said to us, 'Chaps, I have one thing to say...'

Now George shares a birthday with Winston Churchill, and that was the kind of speech we were expecting – all blood, sweat and tears, that sort of stuff. Instead, he said, 'We're going to give out flowers before the game.' Every player had to hand out a bouquet of flowers – we thought he was nuts!

Originally, he was going to have us give them to the Liverpool players, but then he decided that we should run to the four corners of the ground and hand them over to their supporters. It was a brilliant idea, as he wanted to defuse the atmosphere. I wondered if I might be able to nick some, but, as they were large orchids with big ribbons on them, I couldn't do it.

The Boss wanted us to get there early as there would be fewer people around and once we were at the ground there were certain routines to go through. Tony Adams, as captain, would sort out the players' complimentary tickets so they could be left for collection by family or friends. Some players would be sitting in the changing room reading the programme, others would go for a shit. A few players would be being strapped up, but that night, with a massive game ahead of us, it was very, very calm.

There was no negative stuff from George at all. He was very positive as he went around the changing room. There was a quiet confidence about him and he knew that, if there were any signs at all of panic from him, then it would get to the players.

The flowers came into the dressing room, we got a bunch each and went out past the famous 'This Is Anfield' sign on to the pitch alongside Liverpool. We then ran off to different parts of the ground and handed them over to Liverpool fans – I made sure I gave mine to a pretty blonde, of course – and then the match began.

18

There were 41,718 inside Anfield that Friday night of 26 May 1989. There wasn't much room in the dug-out either. We had five members of the coaching staff there, as well as me and the other sub, Martin Hayes. The Boss was up in the directors' box for the start of the game.

For the record, the starting line-ups were: Liverpool – Grobbelaar, Ablett, Staunton, Nicol, Whelan, Hansen, Houghton, Aldridge, Rush, Barnes, McMahon. Arsenal – Lukic, Dixon, Winterburn, Thomas, O'Leary, Adams, Rocastle, Richardson, Smith, Bould, Merson.

The game was being transmitted live on ITV with their top man, Brian Moore, commentating, and people were watching it on television or listening to the radio around the world as both sides have massive followings abroad. It was so late in the season that it was even a nice, balmy night, not the horrible Merseyside weather you usually get.

As you'd expect, the match was played at a high tempo but,

for some reason, we weren't really under a lot of pressure. It certainly didn't seem like they were going to rip us apart. In fact, Steve Bould even had a header cleared off the line by Steve Nicol. I turned to Haysie and said, 'Blimey, we're playing well here.' I was thinking that if we got out with a 0–0 then it wouldn't be a bad result.

George was over the moon at half-time. 'Superb, chaps. Keep calm – we're halfway there.' Then he gave us a bit of advice and said Lee Dixon and Nigel Winterburn should try to get forward and get some crosses into the box, and we should try to get Smudge and Merse into the game a bit more. But you could tell he was really pleased with the way the first 45 minutes had gone. 'Keep it tight,' he said. 'We've not got to chase the game. We will get our chances.'

Liverpool were probably happy with the score as it stood, but they didn't realise that we were more happy. We thought George might change the side and take the sweeper David O'Leary off, but he kept him on and, the way the game was shaping, I remember thinking I might get on. I'd almost forgotten the importance of the game – I was just enjoying the occasion as the second half started. The bench got even more cramped as George decided to move down and take his place on it.

George had said earlier on that it only needed one decent set-piece, and he was right again. After 52 minutes, the referee David Hutchinson gave us an indirect free-kick after Smudge had been fouled by Ronnie Whelan about ten yards outside the box. Nigel Winterburn floated the ball into the area, Smudge got a slight touch with his head and the ball was in the net.

All their players appealed that he hadn't got a touch on it and the goal shouldn't stand. But by that stage they would have appealed for anything: offside, unexploded bomb on the pitch, report of a small earthquake in Peru, you name it. They surrounded the linesman and the referee and for a moment it looked as though the goal might not be allowed. But both the linesman and the referee were nodding towards each other so you could tell they weren't going to disallow it. So another part of George's master plan had worked out.

It was then that the nerves, at last, began. Me and Haysie started to warm up and we reckoned that one of us would be sent on now. But George didn't make any changes: he was happy with the guys on the pitch.

With 15 minutes left, the tension was unbearable. Then Richo put Michael Thomas through for a one-on-one against Grobbelaar. Now Tommo was brilliant in one-on-ones and this was a great chance. So what does he do? He pea-rolled it straight at Grobbelaar, who stopped it easily. Bollocks, I thought, that's our chance gone.

The Boss then decided to take Merse off and send Haysie on. I thought it was scandalous. I had the number 12 on my back and he had 14 – I should have gone on first! The game was becoming more end-to-end and I thought I wasn't going to get on. But then came the message I'd been waiting for – the Boss told me to get my cape off.

Later he would write, 'I went for broke and pulled off Steve Bould so that Perry Groves could join our desperate attack.' Went for broke? Let me think about that... Anyway, the Boss told me to go on and run behind them, down the channels. 'Just keep moving around,' he said. No problem, and on I went.

Even when George had sent Martin Hayes on, he'd still kept the sweeper, but with Bouldie off and me on we went back to 4-4-2. The game was a lot more end-to-end now, and if they scored we would be dead and buried.

I'd been on for about five minutes when there was a tangle between Rodders and their England player Steve McMahon. There was a bit of a ruckus, nothing special, but the whistle went and Rodders went to shake hands with McMahon. Steve must have been riled by their earlier encounter because when Ronnie Whelan arrived on the scene, he and McMahon uncharacteristically said, 'Fuck off, Adams, you're a loser and you always will be.' I thought it was pathetic. Rodders looked at them as if to say, 'What are you talking about, you nuggets?' and I told them to fuck off. Arrogant bastards, I thought. It made you want to stuff them even more.

I had a couple of good touches and took a majestic throw-in, but by now the clock was ticking away. I noticed that McMahon had been asking how long was left and had been given the old one-finger sign from the bench, meaning there was one minute to go.

Then John Barnes got the ball and moved into our left-back area. What he was up to I don't know. Instead of heading towards the corner flag and staying there, waiting to be fouled or something to kill the remaining minute, he tried to beat Kevin Richardson – only for old Chicken Legs to take the ball off him and roll it back to John Lukic.

I was screaming at him to boot it, but he threw it to Dicko. He took a touch and played it to Smudge. He laid it off for Michael Thomas and it took a ricochet. I should say at this point that I then made a fantastic run and took the whole back four with me, honest, leaving a gaping hole for Tommo.

I looked over my shoulder and saw that it was a one-on-one and thought, Thank God, it isn't me. Tommo waited and waited as two Liverpool defenders got closer and Grobbelaar came out. On television, Brian Moore was saying to the watching millions around the world: 'And Arsenal come streaming forward in what will surely be their last attack. A good ball by Dixon, finding Smith, to Thomas, charging through the midfield. It's up for grabs now...'

It sure was. Tommo just flicked the ball over Grobbelaar and it went into the net. Goal number two, and he made it look easy. But the real reason he scored wasn't just his skill or being fit enough to do it so late in the game. It was because he had a massive heart, especially after missing the earlier chance, and once he had got in the penalty area he made the right decision about what to do – that's what separates top players from the ordinary ones. He also had the balls to go for it in the first place.

All hell broke loose as the ball went into the net – and I made a schoolboy error I regret to this day. Tommo did a roll-over, old Bog Brush himself – Nigel Winterburn – was alongside him in seconds to celebrate – what was he doing there? – but I stupidly ran off to the other side of the pitch. I should have been first to congratulate Tommo, then I would have had my picture in the papers the next day. It's a lesson all players have learned these days: head straight for the goalscorer to help him celebrate and you'll be on TV or in the papers too.

Our fans were in the far corner at the end and all our team were going wild in front of them. You could tell by the body language of the Liverpool players that they realised they'd lost it. As I ran back to the halfway line, I said to Steve McMahon, 'Steve, how long to go?' He didn't say anything.

There was just time for me to try to take Steve Nicol out by the knees to waste a bit of time and so I could say that I got booked in a game like that, but I missed. Then Michael Thomas won the ball and headed off towards our goal! All of us wanted him to just boot it away, but he calmly rolled it back to John Lukic and the game was over. We had pulled off Mission Impossible – Arsenal's first title since 1971. And I like to think it was my run that took their defence away from Michael Thomas at the death, so really I won it for us. All right – I'll admit the others played their part too!

I remember David O'Leary went to pick up John Aldridge who had collapsed on the ground, and some of the Liverpool players told him to fuck off, which I still think showed a lack of class. Then we went over to the 4,000–5,000 fans who had followed us and they were ecstatic. In fairness, quite a lot of the Liverpool fans applauded us too.

After that, there was a presentation on the pitch, so George was busy adjusting his tie and shining his shoes on the back of his trouser legs. He was telling us to calm down, but we were flying. When we got back in the dressing room, there was champagne everywhere. Liverpool's Kenny Dalglish and Ronnie Moran popped in and said, 'Congratulations, boys,' and some of their players did too, including John Barnes.

Three of us – me, Merse and Bouldie – were sitting in the corner as everyone was going wild – we were like the old boys from *Last of the Summer Wine*. I looked at the Gaffer and said to them, 'Look at Golden Bollocks over there. Everything he said came true – he must be a warlock.' Then I added, 'He didn't say we would score in the last minute though, so he's useless.'

I worked out that I had come on 19 times as sub that year, as well as the games I had started, and scored some key goals too. I felt I had contributed – I had earned my Championship medal.

We didn't leave the ground until about 11.30pm that night. At that time, there was a booze ban on board coaches, but of course we had crates of lager in among the skips. We got them out as soon as we left Anfield, and even the directors had a drink. Then we realised that no one had made any plans for a proper celebration as we didn't think we were going to win. There were Arsenal fans on the way back down the M6 tooting their horns and waving. I wasn't drunk, but, after a couple of mouthfuls of champagne, you would be flying on the excitement of it all.

We got back to London about 2.30am and someone had radioed ahead that a nightclub – I think was called Winners – out Cockfosters way was being kept open for us. We said to the Gaffer, 'Any chance?' and he said, 'We're all going – let's take the coach.'

Even at that hour there were people on the streets cheering us and inside the club there were birds everywhere – it was mayhem. We all went in and George came in for a drink and then left us to it. Me, I stayed until 6am. Might as well milk it.

The fans wanted your tie, blazer, everything. I gave my tie away, but not the blazer. This was before mobile phones, so I couldn't get hold of Mandy, so I went to Quinny's as he lived near by and crashed out on the settee. I remember waking up about 9.30am and seeing about 15 mad Micks there as well. It turned out he hadn't got a clue who most of them were – he only knew two or three of them – so he left his house full of strangers as we went off to pick our cars up from London Colney and head home.

The following Sunday morning, we all had to meet at Highbury at 10am to go on to Islington Town Hall. These are the great days – everybody loves you and there were 250,000–300,000 on the streets. I was on the Town Hall balcony with the rest of the players and I said, 'Give me the mike!' With microphone in hand I gave them 'Ooh To Be a Gooner' and 'We Are the Champions'. Frank Sinatra had stage presence, but I had balcony presence. Then I started singing, 'My Old Man Said Be a Tottenham Fan,' and the crowd all chanted back, 'Fuck off, bollocks, you're a c—-!' I had them in the palm of my hand.

After that, we all went back to the ground and decided we had to do something, so me, Merse, Bouldie, Smudge and Brian Marwood and all the wives decided to go to TGI Friday's in Covent Garden. Well, we had to take the wives for an airing now and then, didn't we?

19

I started the 1989–90 season playing at Wembley – Wembley FC. There was a pre-season Makita Tournament involving Arsenal, Liverpool, Porto and Dynamo Kiev at Wembley Stadium, but when our squad of 18 was announced I was the only first-team player not named. Instead, I was to play for the reserves, who happened to be just down the road playing Wembley FC, an amateur team.

So on the Saturday I was playing in front of a cow shed – they called it their stand – and listening to the noise from the Stadium in the distance. We won 2–1 and I scored, so I thought, Well, at least I get Sunday off.

The final of the tournament was being played on the Sunday and at 9.30 that morning the phone rang at my home in Colchester. I heard assistant manager Theo Foley's voice on the answerphone asking me to ring him. I didn't answer it on purpose – I wanted them to know that I had probably heard it but couldn't be bothered to call him. There was no way that they could prove I had ignored the message, so I went out to get the papers.

But I'd forgotten to tell Mandy to ignore the phone if it rang again, and when I got back she told me that she had answered the phone and spoken to Theo, so I couldn't pretend I never got the message. Someone had got injured, so I had to get changed and drive to London and then sit on the bench for the final of the tournament and watch us beat Liverpool 1–0. Still, I think I got a £500 win bonus, so it was worth it in a way.

A few days later, before the season really got under way, there was a big trip to the USA as we were playing Independiente of Argentina in the World Club Championship match. I was running around in training a lot because I was keen to make the trip. It sounded great. The game was to be played in the Joe Robbie Stadium in Miami, where the Miami Dolphins played their home games, and I was among the players who headed over there for eight days in West Palm Beach.

When we arrived, the temperature was about 95°F and the humidity was a killer. We started training as we normally did around 10.30am but after about 20 minutes no one could move. As luck would have it George, who had just been divorced, had a bird to see so he was happy for us to start training at 8.30am in future and finish at 10.30am, which meant we had the rest of the day off.

One day, a group of us decided to go to the West Palm Beach Golf Club, which had a course designed by Jack Nicklaus. I think 17 of the 18 holes had water alongside them and the course was surrounded by condominiums with wire mesh around their pools to keep the insects out. The people who lived in them were called snowbirds because they only came down to avoid the snow in winter. They didn't stay there in boiling August, so their homes were all empty.

Me, Rodders, Merse and Martin Hayes could play golf for free as we were a visiting sports team, and when we went to get our clubs and stuff we told the man in the course shop that we hacked around. He reckoned that we would need 25 balls between us in case we lost some. We said bollocks to that and bought 20 each – it wasn't going to break us.

When they said that every hole had water by it, what they really meant was that we would end up playing every hole *in* it. It was like the Dambusters out there. By the sixth or seventh hole, we had practically given up, so we decided to hit our shots into the snowbirds' pools, as it was easier than the course. By the 14th hole we had run out of balls completely – we'd lost all 80. So we ended up playing Wacky Races in the two buggies that we were using. Every time we went past some of the golfers, they waved. How nice. Not really – they were pissed off that we were tearing up their course.

I was losing about 5–6lb in training because of the heat, but when I would go for meals it would put me off to see the Americans eating. All they did was eat, eat, eat. The fat greedy bastards – stuffing themselves with sausages, eggs, waffles and syrup at breakfast and then when we came back after training there would be the same people having their brunch, stuffing themselves again. Unbelievable.

There were loads of American girls around all the time, and, though the American lads didn't like us being with them, that was their problem. We were staying at the West Palm Beach Country Club and every night we were back at some bird's house with a pool. It was like the film *Porky's* every night.

We played Independiente on the Sunday and the match was

beamed live around the world. We beat them 2–1 in front of a crowd of about 10,000 and Rocky scored twice, so we were officially now World Champions. My main memory of that game, though, is the bench. I was sitting on it, as usual, and I must say that it was the best bench I have ever sat on – and I am an expert on the subject. It was air-conditioned, and every 30 seconds or so you would get a blast of cold air up your chuffer. Lovely.

We came back the next day and as pre-season trips go it had been a great holiday. I think the coaches had hoped it would have been a bit like endurance training, but to tell the truth we were fucked. We played Liverpool in the Charity Shield and lost to them. Our first league game as Champions was against Manchester United at Old Trafford. I thought I was right out of the picture, so I was pleased to be named as sub.

As me and Merse went to warm up, there was this pot-bellied geezer in the tunnel in a Manchester United strip playing keepie-uppies. I thought he looked as though he had had a dodgy pre-season, but he was surrounded by cameramen so I said to Merse that we should run out on the pitch behind him. He turned out to be Michael Knighton, a property developer, whose offer to buy United had just been accepted. He went to one end and smashed the ball into an empty net as all these pictures of him were being taken. I just thought, What a knob. His deal to buy United fell through soon after that anyway. Apparently, he didn't have sufficient dinar.

United beat us 4–1 and at one stage I came on for Merse, but we were crap. I think we were still fucked from that week in America.

Back in training at London Colney after that defeat, I went to head a ball, and as I did it felt as though a lift had come down ten floors at top speed and landed on my head. The

England cricket team had a fast bowler called Gladstone Small at that time, and he had no neck to speak of – his head was on his shoulders. I looked like his younger brother as I walked off. The lads were pissing themselves but it was torture. I told our physio Gary Lewin, 'I headed the ball and my neck collapsed into my shoulders.'

I had to go to Harley Street to see a specialist and they put me in a neck brace. It was a freak accident as the muscles around my vertebrae had gone into spasm and fused when I headed the ball. After two weeks, I went back for more treatment as I still felt like Frankenstein. I wanted some manipulation, but the woman who saw me said there was nothing she could do – I would just have to wait.

I was out for four or five weeks in total and I kept thinking that my career was over: I would be Gladstone Small for the rest of my life. The lads kept asking me if I had a coathanger inside my shirt so I was just pleased when my head came out of my shoulders at last. It meant I could start running again – but only in straight lines to begin with.

Still, I got my first full game of the season at Chelsea on 30 September. They had just been promoted and George had decided to shake things up, so I was playing up front and feeling hyped up about it all.

There were over 30,000 at Stamford Bridge but there was no atmosphere – there was a running track around the pitch then. After about ten minutes, I got a throw-in and was chesting it down when Graham Roberts came in from the side. He was a tough defender who'd been at Spurs for years and had played for England. His forearm smashed me right across the face and even though there was no claret my nose was throbbing and my eyes were watering. I thought the referee hadn't seen it and

Roberts was right out of order. Fuck it, I thought, I've got to hurt him.

My chance came after about 20 minutes when he was bringing the ball out of defence. I launched myself at him with one foot over the ball and another foot aimed at his knee joint. I was slightly behind him so I was coming in like a stealth bomber. He wasn't expecting it and I remember some dust coming up as he went down. I went over to give him some abuse but then I saw that he was completely still and I thought, Fuck it – I've killed him. I patted him on the head and he still didn't move. I thought, If he gets up I'm going to have the worst 70 minutes of my life. Part of me wanted him to get up and part of me wanted him to stay down.

Referee Ray Lewis then came over to me and I thought he was going to send me off. I sort of knew him as he worked as a rep for a sports company in the south and he said, 'Perry, you're lucky. I saw what he did to you in the corner and you have reacted to it. If I had not seen that, I would have sent you off. As it is, I'm going to book you.'

The stalks then came on and Roberts was carried off. I had become Public Enemy Number One, and was booed every time I got the ball for the rest of the match. I quite enjoyed it. The game ended 0–0 and as I came off a lot of people were trying to get at me.

In the dressing room, George said, 'Grovesy – top man, top attitude. You didn't let the crowd get you down, you didn't let it ruin your game.' He wasn't saying the tackle was good, just that I had handled it well afterwards. He was saying I'd shown arsehole.

Then there was a knock at the dressing-room door and there was the Old Bill. One of them said, 'Is there a Perry Groves there?' and George said, 'Yes.' The police then said I wasn't to go up to the players' lounge and one of them said, 'We'll escort you to the coach.'

As I walked out, I could see and hear that there were a load of Chelsea supporters waiting for me, and Merse said, 'See you later,' and disappeared. The lads were behind me all right, five per cent.

I had a police officer each side as I went between about 200 fans who were screaming at me and drawing fingers across their necks as if they were slitting my throat. So they put me on the coach, and even our driver fucked off. I had to sit there by myself until everyone else eventually got on board. I had some relatives at the game and they later told me that in the toilets all the talk was Chelsea fans going on about how they would kill me.

Roberts made a bit of a comeback, but he was never the same player again. Years later, I was down at Southampton and not playing because I had done my Achilles, and there was Graham Roberts watching a reserve-team game. I thought, Fucking hell – here we go, and was about to say something when he said, 'All right? What have you done?' I said it was my Achilles, and he said, 'It gets us all in the end.' He was as good as gold. Mind you, I suppose he'd done enough people in his time.

20

A few days after I had sorted out Graham Roberts, we had the second leg of a Littlewoods Cup match at Plymouth. We'd won the first game 2–0 and this time we beat them 6–1 at their place – Michael Thomas got a hat-trick and I got a goal too. By the time we arrived back at London Colney to pick up our cars, it was around 2.30am.

I had a Vauxhall Astra GTE by then and Rodders had a Sierra Cosworth. So Rodders and I decided to start to race around the M25 from Junction 22 to Junction 28 where I would get off and go up the A12. Pretty soon he'd got up to 110mph, so I went past him at 115mph. Rodders had Martin Hayes in with him as a passenger and as I went past they started to wave at me. So I waved back and accelerated away.

Then Rodders came at me again and as he went past they were both still waving at me and mouthing something. I wasn't going to be beaten, so I pulled out and went past one more time with the speedo hitting 120mph. They were still frantically waving at me as I roared away. This was great. I was winning.

The next thing I knew he'd come at me again at around the 125mph mark. I couldn't believe it. But as he went past Rodders put his hazard lights on, cut in front of me and went on the hard shoulder, so I pulled over too. Rodders jumped out of his car, ran up to me and said, 'Fucking hell, Grovesy, you're on fire.'

'Thanks, Rodders,' I said. 'You're doing pretty good yourself.'

'No, you dick,' he interrupted. 'Your engine is on fire!'

I jumped out and we all looked at my engine to see smoke and flames coming from it. Rodders ran back to his car and came back with a little fire extinguisher. I said, 'Thanks,' and looked at him, but he said, 'Fuck off – put it out yourself,' and gave it to me.

So I put the fire out and there we were on the M25 in the middle of the night and my car had had it. They asked me if I was in the AA and of course I wasn't, but Haysie said, 'I am – here's my card.' I went to the breakdown phone – no mobile phones then – and called up for a breakdown lorry. Once I'd done that, the guys went home, leaving me alone to wait for the AA man. All for one and one for all, eh?

Eventually, a low-loader arrived and the driver asked to see my membership card. So I gave him Martin's card and he said, 'It says here that you live at Romford.'

'I'm staying with friends,' I lied. I got in the cab and we headed off to my home in Colchester with my Astra GTE on the back of the lorry. The driver then started saying, 'Martin Hayes... Martin Hayes... I know that name.' He drove on a little bit and then said to me, 'Are you a Gunner?' I said, 'Yep' – that at least was true. But then it got worse.

'You've got a player at Arsenal who used to be with Colchester, he was a right tosser. I support Southend. You lot bought him, and I always thought he was useless.'

I was biting my lip by now, but there was nothing I could say.

Then he said, 'Groves, that was his name, Perry Groves.'

All I could say was, 'Yeah, he's with us.'

On and on he went. 'I suppose he was all right at our level, but not at the top.'

'Yeah, he's pretty crap,' I said.

For 45 minutes, I had to listen to all this as we drove along the M25 and then north up the pitch-black A12. There was nothing I could say – I couldn't let the cat out of the bag. If there was any trouble, he would say that, as I wasn't in the AA, I'd have to get out of the cab, he'd dump my car and I'd be stranded.

Eventually, we got to Colchester and he started to unload my car, so at last I could have my say. 'How do you know Perry Groves was crap? You don't really know about soccer, do you? I'm Perry Groves.'

All the colour just drained out of his face as he tried to think of something to say. Then all he could come up with was, 'You won tonight, didn't you?' I gave him a fiver anyway – at least he had got me home.

When I eventually had the car looked at, the man at the garage was puzzled and said, 'The engine shouldn't have caught fire. How fast were you going?'

I said, 'About 125 mph... for about 20 minutes.'

He just looked at me and later gave me a bill for £800. It was a high-performance car, not an endurance car apparently.

I used to go out with Merse a lot, sometimes to a club in Northolt called Ashtons. One night it was 3am and he asked if I wanted to go to a place called the Silver Orchid. I asked what it was and he said it was a massage parlour. I said, 'OK, let's go for a laugh.'

So we went. It wasn't far, and Merse went in first and I followed him. I had never been to one of these places before, and when we went in it was full of Chinamen sitting there with nothing on but towels around their waists and with a load of birds sitting in the corner. We asked for a price list as all these Chinese blokes were sitting looking at us, but we couldn't stop laughing. We were asking the madam how much for this, and how much for that. We were in there for about 25 minutes and after a while we just said, 'Bollocks – we'll go somewhere else', but we just went home and that was that.

A month later, I got a call to go in and see Ken Friar, a club director, at Highbury. When I got there, he was with George Graham and they looked grim. I wondered what was going on.

'We have got a serious situation here, Perry,' Ken Friar said to me.

'What's that?' I asked.

'You have been frequenting whore-houses.'

'What?!!'

'You have been going to massage parlours.'

'I don't know what you're on about.'

'There were undercover officers inside and out, and it's in court tomorrow.'

It seemed there was one picture of me going in and one of me coming out. It was the only time I had been, and I didn't even get anything! How's your luck?

'We're trying to keep your name out of it,' Ken Friar went on. 'The police have taken statements and say you and another player were frequent visitors and have been there six times.'

'I have been there once,' I insisted. 'We were pissed, no extras and we were in and out in 25 minutes.'

For some reason, they thought the other player was Tony

Adams but I said, 'It wasn't Tony, and I'm not telling you who it was.' If they were going to try to keep names out of it, why would they need to know anyway? Then I started to get the hump. I didn't think they could discipline me for something like that in my private life. I let them know I wasn't having it.

In the end, I didn't hear anything and I forgot all about it. I told Merse what had happened and I was his best mate in the world for a month or so for keeping his name out of it. He was shitting himself and I wondered why he was so worried.

Three months later, we were due to play at Liverpool live on television on a Sunday and had just finished training at London Colney on the Friday before the game. The pitches there are surrounded by fields and in the distance I saw two figures walking down a hill. I thought at first it was a couple of gay boys out and about, but as they got closer I saw that one of them had a camera around his neck and the other was wearing a long coat. The guy in the long, grey coat came up to me and said, 'Perry Groves?' I said, 'Yeah,' and he said, 'We have something we think your wife might be interested in.'

It turned out they were from a Sunday newspaper and they had a signed affidavit that I had been to the massage parlour six times, that I'd had oral sex there, everything. 'What have you got to say?' he asked.

I grabbed hold of the one with the camera and smashed it on the floor and said, 'You fucking sleaze!'

'I'm sure your wife will be interested,' the other one said, as I got in my car and drove away.

I was driving home and thinking about what to do, and I decided to call Eric Hall. I explained what had happened and that one of the papers was on it. 'Tell me the truth,' he said to me, so I did. By the time I got home, I was really wondering what to do. I didn't want Mandy to read it in the papers so I told her about it, that Merse and I were pissed and nothing had happened. 'It's not much of a story, is it?' she said and thought it was all quite funny.

That made me feel better, and the next day I spoke to Eric Hall who said he was trying to sort it out. I also told Niall Quinn who I was sharing a room with, and he pissed himself. Then Eric Hall told me the newspaper said they had affidavits that I tied girls up and whipped them! 'I am going to get you monster money,' he said. 'We'll sue them.'

I phoned Mandy to tell her what was happening and that we might get loads of money from a libel case but I didn't want people to think that I was a pervert.

Quinnie was still pissing himself, but when I told Merse he was just worried about himself. I then went to the Gaffer's room, something you never normally did. I told him what had happened and that something might be in the papers the next day.

'Are you telling me that you are not in the right mental state to play?' he said.

'Of course I'm OK,' I said.

'So what's it got to do with me?' he replied. 'What you do in your private life is nothing to do with me.' But as I left the room he said, 'Thanks for telling me.'

Quinnie wasn't helping much – he kept saying, 'Sex case – hang him' and things like that.

The next morning I was looking in all the newspapers but couldn't see anything when Kevin Richardson started reading from one of them: 'Top London footballers in whore-house...' Kevin then said he knew who the players were – and named two internationals he felt sure were involved, both at another club.

Quinnie then grabbed the paper off him and started reading it too. One of the players, it said, was nicknamed 'The Groper'. After that, Quinnie would call me 'G Roper', after the George Roper character in the *George and Mildred* comedy series. Very funny.

It was only later that I found out the truth. Merse had another mate with red hair, and that mate used to be a regular there. He'd taken Merse with him just to show him what the place was like, nothing untoward happened there and that was why I'd got drawn into it – because they thought this other ginga was me. Thanks, Merse – another one I owe you.

Top: Soaring like an eagle between Nottingham Forest and (England World Cup players) Des Walker (left) and Neil Webb. Rodders watches in admiration.

Middle: Michael Thomas scores the last-gasp title winning goal at Anfield thanks to my brilliant run off the ball, honest! That's me in the distance, far left.

Bottom: My famous Tintin look before I put hair gel on.

The Tuesday Club in training. Getting fit at Highbury on a Tuesday morning... then off on the booze for the rest of the day.

Top: Celebration time. Liverpool defeated at Fortress Anfield – and the party begins.

Bottom: My *Reservoir Dogs* look. That's me in the sunglasses waiting for Rodders to shut up so I can sing to the crowd. I gave them 'Ooh, to be a Gooner' and they loved it.

Oi, barman – two pints of lager, please. Me and Merse celebrating on the field.

Back at Sudbury in my Arsenal strip with my first-born, Lewis.

My sons Lewis
(top, with fair
hair) and Drew in
their Colchester
Royal Grammar
School uniforms.

Top: Thirty up. My 30th birthday party at the Sun pub with mates David Hughes and Peter Whiston (centre).

Bottom: The legend lives on. I float past my mate Steve Whitton – 'Mine's a coffee, waiter' – on the right in a Six-A-Side Masters' tournament.

No 'arm in a shot in my Saints' gear.

21

Being a successful footballer is a great way to have a fantastic sex life. Don't let anyone try and tell you anything different – I should know.

I started out as a little fat ginger kid, all white face and red hair, who the girls didn't want to know. They started noticing me when I was good at football at school and began to hang around me. Mmm, interesting, I thought.

Then I was a Colchester player, followed by the big move to Arsenal and finally getting in the first team at Highbury. Somehow, I got more handsome and sexier every time I progressed up the football ladder. By the time I was in the Gooners' side, I was Robert Redford. Girls are interested in footballers – the fame, the money, the fact they're young and fit and the rest of it, so I thought I'd make the most of it. Most footballers do.

I'd reckon that if you had a squad of 20 footballers you'd find, say, two who are completely true and honest. The rest would be unfaithful to some degree or other, playing around or having full-blown flings.

I compare it to a cricket team. If a side goes out to bat against bouncers, then a couple of them would duck as the ball comes down – the straight-batters I'd call them. Some of the others would try to tuck the ball away for a single and some of them – and that includes me – try to smash the ball out of the ground for six.

I've got to admit that I can't remember a time when I was faithful. It's not a fantastic character trait and it's not something I'm proud of, but I just seemed incapable of being true to one woman or girl. It hadn't been an easy start, mind, as my dad had always warned me against two things – drink and sex. I listened to what he said for the first half of my life, but I've made up for it since. To all intents and purposes, I was teetotal until I was 21, but I've got bladdered enough since then. And as for the girls...

Dad was right, of course. Not in the old-fashioned way of it sapping your strength, but he was worried they would take up so much time that I wouldn't be able to concentrate on football. Well, he wasn't quite right there. Pity he didn't tell me never to score for Arsenal – I'd have ended up breaking every goalscoring record the club has.

As I've said, I lost my virginity when I was 16, and after that we were at it morning, noon and night. You could say I was a sex addict, although I think all this addiction thing is bollocks. I just liked it, simple as that. But it was non-stop for me from there on, two or three times a day. Before training, after training and one at night just to round the day off.

I was married to Mandy from 1986 until 1996 and I was unfaithful throughout. Now the obvious conclusion is that I was unhappy in the marriage – but that couldn't be more wrong. I was happy with Mandy – if I hadn't been, my football career wouldn't have gone so well – but I wanted to have my cake and eat it too. In fact, I wanted to own Mr Kipling's factory.

Mandy was completely blameless. She didn't play around, she was attractive and a great mother. We had a good sex life too. She even liked football, for goodness sake! None of it was because I was unhappy in the marriage. Psychologists can say whatever nonsense they like – it was simply that I couldn't resist temptation.

While I was at the Gunners and married to Mandy, I was going out with two sisters. They were both attractive, both stunners, really good looking. Oh, and they were both married too. I know it was asking for trouble really, but the one thing I'd say about them and all the others is this – it takes two to tango. No one did anything they didn't want to, and no one was forced into anything. If it became known, then I would take all the blame. Fair's fair.

Each of these sisters knew I had dated the other one, but they were unaware that I was doing it at the same time – both thought my relationship with the other was in the past. In fact, what was happening was that I'd see one of them and before, during and after the shenanigans she would ask, 'Who was the better, me or her?' I would say, 'You, of course.' A couple of weeks later, I would see the other sister and she would ask me exactly the same question, so I would give her the same answer: 'You're miles better.'

I know I was asking for trouble, as, even though the town where they lived is a big place, it has a village mentality. By that, I don't mean it is full of idiots, just that everyone seems to know what everyone else is doing. You might also wonder why I would see married women. I reckon that, if you are going to have an affair, you're better having it with someone who is married, because they have as much to lose as you do. If only one of you is married, then that person is vulnerable, while the other person who is single is in a position of power.

I was seeing the sisters on and off for about a year, perhaps a year and a half, but it eventually petered out as I started seeing our nanny. I was running out of time to see them all, wasn't I? I even had it away with the mother of one of the Arsenal players. She would have been about 45 then and I was in my twenties, but she looked good. It wasn't a one-off with her – it was a two-off actually. And, before you start trying to work out which player it might have been, it wasn't one of the household names. It was one of the younger pros, and we had quite a few of those during my time there.

My main affair during that time was with Jenny, a lovely blonde I had met at Stringfellows. We had a fling that lasted for 18 months during my spell at Arsenal and then again when I was transferred to Southampton. She's moved on in life since, so I don't want to embarrass her or her family by giving her real name. I am a little bit of a gentleman like that – just.

We had some great fun together, and she'd often stay at hotels with me when she could. Once Arsenal were at the Noke Hotel in St Albans on a Saturday night in preparation for a Sunday match. I wasn't going to be playing so I thought it would be great if Jenny came round. The only problem was that I roomed with Paul Merson and I didn't want him in the room while I was having my evil way.

Eventually, I persuaded him to go to Gary Lewin, the physio, and say that, as I had a cold, he didn't want to catch it and could he have a room of his own. It worked, so straight away I was on the phone to Jenny and she drove round the M25 from

Romford in next to no time. We had a great session, interrupted only by Merse who kept ringing up, asking me if he could come and watch 'just for ten minutes'. He kept going on about how I owed him because look what he had done for me. I told him to get lost, of course, and everything seemed to have worked out to perfection.

But, as always, things got complicated. At about 2am, Jenny and I were lying in bed when the fire alarm went off. I put my head out of the door and there was the manager running up and down, saying there had been a fire in the kitchen and everyone had to get out. Normally, these things are false alarms, but this was for real.

Fucking hell, I thought, if I'm caught I'm really for it. I'd be fined, the club might boot me out for breach of discipline, Mandy might get to hear about it – the works. So, quick as a flash, I told Jenny to put on my Arsenal tracksuit and my baseball cap. Then I shoved her on to the fire escape and told her to make a dash for it. As she legged it away from the hotel, I could hear the manager shouting after her, 'Sir! Excuse me, sir...'

We all had to gather on the car park for a head count and Merse – it would be him – had told the others what was going on. They were pissing themselves, but it was the dead of night in November and I was standing there freezing in boxer shorts and a vest while they had tracksuits on. The hotel manager told George Graham and Gary Lewin that one of the players had left the hotel so they did a head count.

'No, they're all here,' they told him, but the manager insisted he had seen a player leaving. By now the rest of the side were in hysterics and winding the Gaffer up, saying 'Who can it be?' and all that stuff. I was shivering and kept chipping in, 'No, no, we're all here!' The rest of the lads deliberately kept asking me why I hadn't got my tracksuit on, so I told them it was because I'd left in such a hurry I hadn't had time to put it on.

The hotel management even looked in the car park but couldn't see anyone. That was because Jenny, clever little thing, had got in her car, put the driver's seat down and laid flat on it so she couldn't be spotted.

Eventually, we were all allowed back in the hotel. Panic over. Two hours later, there was a knock on the door. Jenny had come back to the hotel and said to me, 'Do you think I should go home?'

'Good idea,' I said. I'd had enough by then and just wanted to get to sleep. But I made sure she left the tracksuit – it would have looked funny if that had disappeared.

Later, when I was transferred from Arsenal to Southampton, the club put me in the Hilton Hotel there for three months while I was, in theory, looking for a home for Mandy and myself and our two young boys. I just looked at it as being a bachelor again for three months. What man wouldn't? Whenever Mandy mentioned coming down, I'd come up with reasons why she shouldn't. I mean, who would look after the dog back home? But Jenny would be coming down all the time – it was great.

And then it all went sour. I never gave Jenny my home number, just the mobile, but one day she'd got hold of my mobile phone bill. She'd gone through it and noted the Colchester number I'd rung most and worked out that this must be my home number. Crafty or what? Perhaps you can guess what came next.

I was back home for the weekend and it was one o'clock on Sunday morning and I was lying in bed with Mandy when the phone rang. For the first few rings, I was asleep, and by the time it woke me up properly, the answerphone had kicked in. I heard Jenny's voice and a chill came all over me as she said, 'Hi, Mandy, this is someone who knows your husband really well.'

I was out of the bed in a flash. I might have been quick on the field, but that was the fastest I'd moved in years. There was one problem – I didn't know how the answerphone worked. I couldn't stop it. I was standing there in my boxer shorts with my life flashing before my eyes as Jenny, who was obviously pissed and had decided to go for broke, went on, 'There's something you should know...'

By then I was trying to open the phone to rip the little micro-tape out, but I couldn't even do that.

Mandy had woken up by now and was asking what was going on. I eventually managed to stop the bloody answerphone but the damage had been done, so I went on the offensive. I became the injured party and put on my angry act.

'Mandy,' I said, 'I have not got a clue what that was all about. Some silly bird thinks it's funny to make a call like that at this time in the morning. I can't believe someone would do that.' I was so outraged that for a second – well, a fraction of a second – I almost believed my lies myself.

On Monday, I fronted Jenny up about it, but she denied it was her. I knew it was, though – I recognised her voice, for goodness sake – and I thought, This is going to be dangerous. I was right.

Mandy and the boys then moved down to the Southampton area, so I started seeing less and less of Jenny and that suited me. I was hoping that it would eventually peter out and there'd be no blood on the wall. Eventually, I decided to end it and that would be that. I told Mandy I was doing a presentation at Romsey FC near Southampton on the Friday night – the sort of thing the pros do at amateur clubs all the time, a little bit of good public relations. Instead, I drove to London determined to end it, and I did. I told Jenny our affair had to stop and, the deed done, drove back to Southampton. I got home about 11.30pm and went to bed, feeling pretty pleased with myself for managing to get out of it all without too much problem. Talk about wishful thinking.

The next morning I woke up and Mandy was standing over me by the bed. 'Was the presentation good last night?' she asked.

'Yes,' I said. 'It went all right.'

'What sort of age group was it?' she went on.

I really should have realised what was around the corner, but, as always, I soldiered on. 'Oh, ten- to 16-year-olds, you know.'

Then came the killer question. 'How far is it to Romsey?'

'About five miles or so.'

Then she looked me in the eye and said, 'I've just checked your mileage and you did 217 miles last night. What's that about?'

I was bang to rights, but I floundered on. 'No, you don't understand,' I said. 'It was the London branch of Romsey FC – it was a presentation up in town.'

Yes, I know, it was the most feeble lie you could ever think of – that a small-town team from Hampshire would have a presentation evening in London, but I was desperate.

It didn't wash for a second.

'It wouldn't be that tart who was on the answerphone, would it?' Mandy asked.

So I came clean. Just my luck – caught out on the very morning after I'd ended the affair. There really is no justice. Another girl I had been seeing – well, I did say I couldn't be faithful, didn't I? – had told Mandy about the mileage trick so she could check to see if I had been going where I'd said I was.

But I got what I deserved. I had put my marriage in jeopardy for the sake of a shag – it was as simple as that. When you have an affair, you only think about yourself. You don't think about the hurt to other people and their family. You never think that you're going to get caught so you end up taking more and more chances. That means more people end up knowing, and that means it won't stay a secret forever. And, if you do get caught, then after four or five months you start to think about doing it all again!

I'd had flings before but it wasn't going to come out because the other women had husbands or boyfriends, so they had as much to lose as me. Now I realised that I had jeopardised everything Mandy and I had worked for. She had been trustworthy and didn't deserve what I had done to her. The truth was I wasn't mature enough to get married in the first place. The only advice I'd give from all of this is that a bloke should wait until he's 30 or so, then get married.

22

There was only one league game when I scored twice for Arsenal, and I can hardly remember a thing about it. We played Manchester City at home in October 1989 and I was up front alongside Alan Smith, with Brian Marwood playing wide. Early on, Lee Dixon hit a right-foot screamer, but the only thing it hit was me – smack on the forehead. It was like a sledgehammer. I'd have been a lot safer in goal for Manchester City if Dicko was shooting.

I was dazed and still can't remember what happened after that. Apparently, our physio Gary Lewin came on and asked questions like, 'How many fingers am I holding up? What's your wife's name?' – all the usual stuff. After the game, I had a shower and said to Michael Thomas, 'What was the score?' and he said 4–0 to us. Then I asked him who had scored and he said, 'You got two.' They should have knocked me out for every game!

For the record, I scored with a diving header in the first half and then – after being knocked out – scored again in the second half. I never again got two for the Gunners, or anyone else come to that, so it's a shame I can't remember much about it. I had to get all the papers the next day to find out what had happened in the game.

You wouldn't bet on me to score twice all that often, but a lot of footballers will bet on virtually anything. There was a payphone in the hall at Highbury and we were always using it to place bets. We didn't want to be seen putting the bets on, so we would get someone to do it for us. Paul Merson has spoken about his betting habits a lot, but I liked a bit of a bet too, although nothing like Merse.

Footballers will always say publicly they don't bet on football games – it's meant to be illegal. But that's a load of bollocks. Of course they bet on games. We did it a lot. We'd never bet against ourselves, though – we'd always bet on us to win.

One of the best bets I had involved Arsenal players and the 'who would score' odds you get at the bookies. Michael Thomas was our usual penalty-taker but he had missed a couple, so we decided to change and Lee Dixon said he would take them. Now Dicko was a full-back and he hardly ever scored, so I got odds of 25–1 against him scoring. What no one knew, apart from the Arsenal players, was that as our new penalty-taker his odds should have been a lot shorter. I put £50 on him and he came up trumps. That was a nice earner for me as I picked up £1,250 on the bet.

When spread betting came in, the players were always keen on having a bet on what time the first booking would be, throw-in, goal – anything like that. I remember in 1994 Mandy and I stopped at Merse's house on the day of the World Cup Final. The game between Italy and Brazil was on TV but he hardly watched it. He kept running in and out between the rooms looking at all the sets and getting on the phone. It turned out he had got a bet on, but not a normal bet. It was all linked to who scored, what numbers were on the goalscorers' backs and so on – you could even buy or sell on bets during the match. Merse worked harder during that game than he did during some games at Highbury.

In December 1989, we played Manchester United. They'd signed Gary Pallister from Middlesbrough for £2.3 million, a British record transfer fee, but I was too quick for him and gave him the runaround. I got the only goal of the game too – a left-foot volley into the corner of the net – in the 15th minute and even George Best, who was doing the expert commentary on television, said I'd played well. He knew a player when he saw one!

Just before Christmas, we played Glasgow Rangers at Ibrox in something called the Zenith Data Systems Challenge Trophy, or, to put it more simply, the British club Championship. There weren't many Arsenal fans there when I came on as sub, but we ended up winning 2–1 in front of a crowd of about 31,000. I was glad I got on, because the one thing I didn't want was to have to play in the reserves the next day.

I was still in and out of the side, most often being sub, and whenever I was dropped I would think it was out of order. I'd go and see the Boss at the training ground and the conversation would go something like this:

'I want to see you,' I would say, and then something like, 'Such-and-such is worse than me. I'm playing well and I think you're wrong.'

'Grovesy,' George would reply, 'I agree with everything you've said. But I'm the manager, so tough.'

At least I had put my point across. Then I'd say, 'Thanks, Gaffer' and he would say, 'You're still part of my plans.' I would always feel better after meetings like that, although when I asked about a transfer a couple of times he just said, 'Don't be silly.'

I wasn't stupid – I had seen big names go to war with him and what had happened to them. They would end up in the reserves and training with the youth team. I knew that he was the Guv'nor and I could only go so far. Remember I was his first signing and I think he was like most managers who sign someone – they want that player to do well because, among other things, it shows they had good judgement in the first place. But sentiment never got in the way – he dropped me enough times to show that!

One player who got busy, as they say, in his dealings with George was Brian Marwood. He had signed from Sheffield Wednesday in March 1988 and played wide left in our Championship side and collected a medal, although he missed the Liverpool game because of injury. But he got carried away as he was also the Professional Footballers Association rep at the club. He got an office in St Albans with a phone and a chair and called himself something like Brian Marwood Inc. He later became PFA chairman and a commentator on Sky, but after we'd won the title he got involved with the Gaffer over money. He felt our bonuses should go up the next season. The system was that at the start of a new season you agreed to the bonus payments that coming year. If you didn't sign the bonus sheet, you wouldn't get paid the bonuses.

We were all at Highbury one day and we said to Brian, 'You go and see them,' and off he went to see Ken Friar and George Graham. He came back and said to the squad, 'Don't sign your bonus sheets.' He loved the union aspect and he called a union meeting in the coaches' room at Highbury.

Then George came in the room and said, 'Who the hell has got a problem? You cheeky bastards! Who here doesn't want to play in the first team? Raise your hands if you don't want to sign.'

Brian put his hand up, but no one else did. We all said something like, 'It's the first we've heard about it.' George just told us to get the sheets signed and stormed out of the room.

Brian just said, 'Thanks a fucking lot. You're all frightened of him.' No one could meet his eye. We were all behind him – five per cent.

A little while later Brian was transferred to Sheffield United after just two and a half years at the club. He had been one of the most pivotal players in the side while he was with us, but I think in the end he hung himself – or should I say we hung him.

George was later to write, 'I could not hide from him the fact that I thought he was giving too much time to union matters to the detriment of his football... He can look back with pride on what he achieved with Arsenal, even if he did not always agree with the manager.'

That year we were drawn away in the FA Cup at Stoke, the club from which Arsenal had bought both Lee Dixon and Steve Bould. Around this time, one of the bits of fun we used to have was when we saw someone wearing a wig – we called it our rug alert. If we saw someone with a dodgy syrup, you would start to make a siren sound, a sort of 'wah-wah' noise, to let everyone else know.

As we sat on the coach waiting to leave Stoke's Victoria Ground, I saw a man alongside who looked as though he had a cat on his head, never mind a wig. I immediately started going 'wah-wah' and the other lads had a look. They all started laughing, but for some reason or other Bouldie was completely pissing himself. We even said to him, 'It's not *that* funny.'

But then this geezer, with his bright-ginger wig, got on board our coach, so the 'wah-wah' started again. He started to walk down the aisle and I thought, Blimey – he's got some front to get on board. Then he went up to Dicko and said, 'Well played,' and Dicko said to him, 'Thanks, Dad.' Oh no! We'd been taking the piss out of Dicko's father!

After he got off the coach, Dicko said to us, 'The thing is, he thinks that no one notices.' His father came to see us whenever we played in that area, but we never made the same mistake again – at least not to his face.

By March 1990, the goals had dried up and we hadn't scored for six games, so the Boss had me in the starting line-up against Nottingham Forest at Highbury. I was to play wide on the right, which was fine by me, apart from the fact that Forest's left-back was England's Stuart 'Psycho' Pearce. Before the game Merse, who was playing on the left, kept saying to me, 'You're against Psycho – all the best,' and stuff like that. But then George said to us, 'If things aren't working out, you two can swap.'

I was being clattered from the start so I said to Merse, 'Let's swap' and he said, 'No way.' Then I told him that George had said we should swap, and as we ran past each other to change wings he just said to me, 'Cheers, you fucking knob.' Of course, Psycho larruped him everywhere, and every time he did him I was laughing my head off on the other side of the pitch. Merse was calling out, 'Grovesy! Swap?' every five minutes! I scored before half-time and we went on to win 3–0, but I came off at the break as I was injured, leaving Merse to take his punishment like a man. I wouldn't call Psycho a dirty player, by the way, but he did intimidate opponents and anyone less brave or shrewd than him would be in big trouble.

I was in trouble myself when we played at Liverpool at Highbury that season. I felt my Achilles tendon tighten and I couldn't run. I went down and practically crawled off the pitch.

Gary Lewin ran around and looked at me and said he didn't think it was a calf injury, so it could be my Achilles.

It was soaking wet and these two old St John's Ambulancemen came to help me get back to the dressing room. I don't know how old these two were, but one looked about 85 and the other looked around 90. They put me on a chair with wheels and strapped me in so I couldn't move, and then this pair of twats set off pushing me around the ground in the pouring rain.

Worse was to come. The back wheel of the chair caught on the corner of the pitch where it was raised above the level of the track alongside it, and I toppled over, right in front of the Liverpool fans in the corner at the Clock End. My face landed in a puddle and I got burns from being dragged along the track. I couldn't move as I was strapped in, and I thought I might drown on national television. The Liverpool fans loved it and were calling out to me in that loveable Scouse way they do.

I must have been there for about 30 seconds, although it seemed like ages before they eventually managed to get me upright again. All the players who weren't on the pitch were in the dug-out or the paddock area, and they were watching this and pissing themselves. Another OAP joined the two who'd been in charge of me so far, and eventually the three of them got me up the steps that lead to the tunnel and into the changing room.

The club doctor came to see me, took one look and said, 'Lift him up,' so I could go on the treatment table. These senile bastards said, 'One, two, three... lift,' but couldn't budge me. Then they tried again, with the same result. 'Is this Jeremy Beadle or something?' I said, and they said, 'What?' So I pointed out, because they were obviously too stupid to realise it, that I was still strapped in the chair. No wonder they couldn't lift me up.

Oh, the joys of being a football star!

23

I ended up being out for three or four weeks and that was the first indication that something might be wrong with my Achilles tendon. But on 6 April 1990, the biggest thrill of my life occurred when my son Lewis Drew Groves was born.

First of all, I would advise any bloke who is trying to start a family not to tell his mates. That's what I did at Arsenal before he was born, and pretty soon they were all asking, 'Need a hand?' or leaving milk bottles with a little bit of water and milk in them so it looked like Harry Monk, or saying they could pop round, etc.

We'd been in Sweden on a pre-season trip in July 1989 when Mandy telephoned me and said she thought she was pregnant, adding, 'But don't tell anyone.' So I called a team meeting in Gary Lewin's physio room – well, I wanted to get them off my back – and told them the good news. Most of them said, 'Who's the father?' but I like to think they were joking.

Mandy went to the maternity hospital in Colchester where she worked to have the baby on the first Thursday in April. She was told she had a couple of hours at least before anything would happen, so I went to a nearby golf course and played nine holes. When I got back, she was upset because they wanted to discharge her – they didn't think it was due for a while. But she said, 'No, I'm having the baby now – I know I am,' and I said she was staying. We had a big row with the doctors but she stayed, and, sure enough, early on Friday my son was born. I remember when he came out into the world I was counting legs and arms to make sure everything was fine, and even when he was on Mandy's chest I didn't know if the baby was a boy or girl.

If we're being honest, I think 90 per cent of blokes would want their first-born to be a son, so I was double-chuffed that it was a boy and healthy. It changed me, because until then I had been an only child with just football and the rest of it. And then one day you realise you are not the most important thing in the world after all.

That season we had a home game against Southampton, and in their side was Russell Osman, who had played for Ipswich and England. I went on for about ten minutes with George's 'go and run around' instructions and although we had been losing 1–0 we ended up winning 2–1 and I had been a nuisance as instructed. After I'd changed I went to meet my dad and he said there was some bloke looking for me. What goes round comes round, they say, and it turned out to be Jonathan Crisp, the chairman from Colchester who'd thought I was crap. He was looking for Osman, who it seemed was his best mate.

'Well done,' he said. 'I'm glad to see you are doing well.'

'No, you're not,' I said. 'You're not pleased to see I'm doing well at all.'

'It's water under the bridge,' he said. Then he explained what he wanted. 'Can you get me into the players' lounge or ask Russell Osman to get me in?'

I just said, 'Leave it to me...' He could still be waiting there for all I know.

Liverpool won the Championship that season and we came fourth. Our last game of the season was at Norwich and it was a boiling hot May weekend. We went up the day before and stayed at some sports village or other, and all the players went for a walk the night before the game. There were lots of Arsenal fans up there, corporate hospitality people and the like and loads of people who recognised us as we went for our stroll. They wanted us all to come and have a drink with them at a bar in the complex, but we didn't want to as it was the night before a game.

Eventually, they sent out 13 or 14 pints of lager shandy or soft drinks to all of us and we sat outside and had one drink each. Most of the players moved off but five of us stayed behind – Kevin Richardson, Nigel Winterburn, Bouldie, Merse and me, just having a chat. Then, out of the corner of my eye, I saw George, Gary Lewin and some of the other coaching staff walking towards us. 'Fuck,' I said, 'here comes Gaddafi.'

They all said, 'So what?'

So I said, 'Just look at the table.'

There in front of us were 14 empty glasses – it looked as though us five had been having a session. We had a choice to run or stay but as Bouldie said, 'It's not as though he doesn't know who we are, is it?'

Gary Lewin and Stewart Houston walked past and then George came by and said, 'Evening, chaps,' and then, 'It's always the same old faces.'

'Bollocks,' I said after he'd gone. 'We're all going to be dropped.'

But nothing more was said and we ended up drawing the

game 2–2. On the coach going back after the game, I said, 'He must be going soft.' I was wrong.

With the season over, we all flew to Singapore the next day for a game against South Korea, and then we were all due to go to an island called Batam for an end-of-season jolly. Bouldie didn't make the trip because he was injured, but the rest of us played and we beat South Korea 2–1. Then we went out on the town and met up with some air stewardesses and went back to their hotel, Raffles.

The next day I was expecting to head off to this holiday island when I got a phone call in my room to see Ken Friar in the hotel foyer. I said, 'Just me?' but Merse had to go too. When we got down there, Nigel and Richo were already waiting. Then Ken Friar came up and gave us our passports. 'Mr Graham will deal with you when you get back,' he said. 'It's to do with a breach of club discipline.'

All the other lads were outside in the coach getting ready to go off for their break. As they pulled away, they were pulling faces, waving and taking the piss, and we had to fly back to London. We went club class, but I don't think any of us had a drink all the way back. We didn't feel in the mood – naughty boys and all that. When we landed, it was on the front page of the papers, but we told the reporters it was nothing really as we came through Heathrow. I had to tell my dad it was nothing as well.

A week later, I had to report to the ground to see the Gaffer, and I travelled in on the train and tube. When I got to Highbury, there were loads of reporters and cameramen there and they all wanted to know what I was going to say to George. I went in to see him in his office in one of the executive boxes, but over his shoulder I could see where the new stand was being built, and all the ground staff were doing cartwheels on the pitch because they knew that I could see them.

So I was trying not to smirk as George was saying, 'Serious breach of club discipline... same old faces...' Then he asked me who the other players were who'd been with us five but I said I wasn't going to tell him. He said, 'Bouldie has told me anyway', so I said, 'It doesn't matter then.' I wasn't going to fall for that old trick.

George said he was originally going to fine me two weeks' wages but had decided to make it one instead. Then he told me to go out of the back door to avoid the press.

'No, I'm going out of the front', I said. I was going to milk the publicity. I went out and they all grabbed me. 'He's been hard but fair', I said. I knew George would like that.

24

The Boss had been busy bringing in new players during the summer ready for the 1990–91 season. He'd bought centre-back Andy Linighan from Norwich for £1.25 million and the Swedish international Anders Limpar from Cremonese in Italy for around the same price. But the biggest talking-point was signing David Seaman from QPR for £1.3 million, then a world record fee for a goalkeeper. John Lukic was a big favourite with the fans and had never let us down, but George wanted to replace one very good goalkeeper with an even better one.

On their first day at our training ground, Seaman and Linighan were as quiet as little boys on their first day at a new school. We decided to call David Seaman 'H'. Most people think it was from 'Harry Monk', which rhymes with spunk, as his name was Seaman, but in fact it was from 'Harry the Head' because of the size of his head. Footballers get funny nicknames, I know.

'H' was under massive pressure to show that he was better

than Lukey and whenever he missed something in training I'd call out, 'Lukey would have got that' – as a joke, you understand. Although 'H' was about 6ft 3in, he wasn't as tall as Lukey, but he had massive presence. Although the fans weren't too happy at the start, he went on to become one of the finest goalkeepers in Arsenal history and a regular in the England team for years.

Andy Linighan was a good player too, but he had a hard job getting into that Arsenal back four. To begin with, Steve Bould was there, and later on Martin Keown came back to the club, so he didn't play as often as he would have liked.

As for Anders Limpar – he was going to be playing wide on the left, so it looked as though I was going to be his stuntman. In August, we were in the Makita Tournament at Wembley again and he scored a great goal against the other English team playing, Aston Villa. The fans loved him immediately.

That season we were second-favourites for the title at 7–1 – Liverpool were the bookies' choice. Our first game of the season was at Wimbledon. They were the bully boys of the time with their Crazy Gang reputation and all that, but George came up with a way of keeping their main striker John Fashanu quiet. The Boss knew him from their Millwall days together and said, 'He has this reputation for attitude and being a bully, but he's not the brightest. I'm going to put it around that I'm interested in him.' He also said that we should mention this to Fash before and during the game.

Normally, Fash was the sort of player who sharpened his elbows before a game, but Bouldie and Rodders were nice to him and said things like, 'Well done, big fella,' during the game and totally psyched him out. Not that he did much right during the match – he had a stinker. I'm not saying that he didn't try as hard as usual, but what we had done was take that attitude element out of his game.

We ended up winning 3–0 and I came off the bench and scored the last goal in the 90th minute, a 20-yard half-volley into the top corner. But really I was playing to get away. I'd heard that Manchester City were interested in me and I had a phone call from a journalist on the Manchester evening paper asking me about it. 'Yes', I said, 'I'd love to join them. They're a big club, I'm in my mid-twenties and I want to play regularly' – all that stuff. In training, I'd be singing 'Blue Moon', Manchester City's theme tune, and 'Please Release Me, Let Me Go'.

Then George called me in and said, 'It's been funny for two weeks, but give it up now, will you?' Earlier in the year, he'd sold Niall Quinn to City for about £700,000 and he was doing really well up there. It looked as though the Boss might have let him get away cheaply. 'They're not going to have another one for nothing', he said. 'I don't know if you are going or when you are going or where you are going. One thing's for sure – you ain't going to Manchester City'. He obviously wasn't going to make the same mistake twice.

We played Everton away and I came on, scored and we drew 1–1 and I played all right. Then Anders was on international duty for Sweden so it was stuntman time again. I was chosen to start a Rumbelows Cup match against Chester and I scored twice. The Man of the Match in that game was going to be awarded a television as a prize, and I was out there thinking about where I was going to put it and how would I rearrange the furniture. Then Merse went and scored a great goal with a fantastic chip, so he got the award. He went on for ages about how good it was and that it had teletext and everything. Total injustice.

Still, I had scored four goals and it was early in the season, but I knew that once Anders came back from Sweden he'd be straight back into the side. It was great for George, but not so good for me, as I wasn't getting a look in really.

On 20 October, we played Manchester United at their place in what was to become known as The Battle of Old Trafford. We were in second place behind Liverpool, so we needed a good result against United and I was sub again. There was already bad blood between the teams dating back to when Nigel Winterburn took the piss out of Brian McClair for missing a penalty, and this match turned out to be the famous game that brought it all out in the open. The one person you can't blame is me, though. I was laughing my head off while it happened.

We'd scored first through Anders, who'd seen that their keeper Les Sealey was out of position and took advantage of it. Sealey scooped the ball out of the net, but the referee Keith Hackett was fantastic. He was perfectly positioned to see that it had gone over the line and, although a lot of referees would have bottled it, he gave the goal.

Then in the 60th minute Anders nutmegged their Irish full-back Denis Irwin, and they had a go at each other. Nigel Winterburn steamed in and he ended up on the ground. Next McClair and Irwin waded in while he was on the floor. Anders punched McClair and then the Three Degrees arrived on the scene: Rocky, Paul Davis and Michael Thomas. McClair was not happy I can tell you when those three got involved. In seconds, it had turned into a 21-man brawl – only David Seaman wasn't involved. But there was more to come.

As it went on, both benches decided to join in – apart from me. The Gaffer, David O'Leary, who was our other sub, and Stewart Houston from our side plus United manager Alex Ferguson and his assistant Brian Kidd were at it too. In fairness, I think they were trying to calm it down, as were some of the players. As for me, I always believed in having a pair of glasses handy to put on in case there was a fight like that. I couldn't be arsed to get involved either. I thought it was hilarious.

There were headlines in the papers and the FA fined both clubs, but if that happened now McClair and Irwin would be suspended for months, Anders would have been off, and I don't know what they would have done to Nigel.

As it was, five of our lads were docked two weeks' wages by the club and George had the idea for Arsenal to fine him £10,000 just to show that the manager must carry the can for his side's behaviour. Publicly George said he couldn't condone the behaviour of his players, but at a team meeting afterwards he said, 'Fantastic.' It wasn't that he approved of the brawl, he didn't, but he knew that if he had that sort of team spirit then we stood half a chance. It had been all for one and one for all – apart from me on the bench, of course.

Both clubs were eventually fined £50,000 and we had two points deducted and they had one taken off them. I think we got the heavier punishment because we'd been in trouble with the FA a year earlier after it had all gone off in the tunnel after a match. After all those fines and wages being docked and everything, I told the lads I'd organise a whip-round for them, but I never did.

At the end of October, we had a tricky Rumbelows Cup game at Maine Road against Manchester City, who'd had a good start to the season. The Boss left David Rocastle out and I played wide right, my favourite position. I scored the first goal after 50 minutes, a tap-in from a Paul Merson cross, but, as I peeled away in front of our fans to celebrate in style, I slipped and fell over like a clown on a banana skin. We ended up winning 2–1, and I got booked as well, but I thought, as I'd already scored five goals and it wasn't even November yet, I was on course for 20 that year. As it turned out, I didn't score again until the last day of the season!

We were doing all right, but Liverpool were really flying. At one stage, we were eight points behind them, and that two-point deduction hadn't helped. So George decided to call a meeting – it was the siege mentality kicking in. 'This is the best start this club has had in 40 years and if you read the newspapers you'd think it was the worst,' he said, and made it clear it was us against the world. 'They love it, having a go at Arsenal.'

Everyone was writing us off, but the week after the points deduction we played Southampton. I started, made two, and we won 4–0. Then it was off to Marbella.

There must have been a gap in the fixtures because George had arranged the trip for bonding and so on. I thought of it as a bit of a jolly-up. We stayed at one of the big hotels on the coast, and one day Merse said, 'Fancy going to a country club where some of the villains go? There's some heavy people there, so don't go too leery. My uncle knows them – it's run by some bloke called Freddie Foreman.'

'It can't be,' I said, but he insisted it was.

Freddie Foreman was a pal of the Krays who was eventually jailed for being an accessory after the fact in the East End murder of Jack 'The Hat' McVitie.

I said we should take Alan Smith and Lee Dixon with us, and the four of us set off up the hills to this club that Freddie ran. Freddie came out to meet us and took us inside and it was full of blokes with Mars Bars – scars – on their faces. We were very, very polite and said, 'How do you do?' to everyone.

Freddie then introduced us to his son Jamie, who is now a well-known actor, and for five or six hours they looked after us superbly. We had a full Sunday roast with all the trimmings, just like being back in the East End. There were loads of birds around too, and they looked all right, but we weren't stupid. They were all being nice to us so we showed them respect – I didn't want to have my kneecaps shot off. It was an eye-opener for Dicko and Smudge, I can tell you.

The rest of the time, we'd spend the nights at Puerto Banus and that was where I first became aware of 'charlie' – cocaine. We'd be out all night and other people around us would be disappearing to the toilets and then come back and start bouncing around. At around 3am or 4am, I would be seeing the world though hazy eyes, but everyone else seemed great. 'They have a toot in the khazi and come out right as ninepence', Merse told me. The players weren't on it, though, and, even though Merse later admitted he had a cocaine problem, he wasn't on it then.

Merse did, however, have his problems with gambling. He once asked me if I could lend him some money. 'Sure', I said. 'How much?'

'Five', he said.

'Let's go to a cashpoint and I'll get you a monkey out.'

'No, five grand – and I have to have it by 2pm.'

I told him I could go to my building society in Colchester, which was an hour away, but he said, 'I have to have it by 2pm – you're no good to me now.'

Whether he went to the club or what I don't know, but the next day he said to me, 'It's all sorted. I'm not going to put myself through that again.'

Sometimes when we were both injured at the same time we couldn't go running, so we'd be put on mountain bikes and told to go for an eight-mile ride instead. Merse would ask, 'How long will that take?' and I said about half an hour. 'Great', he said. 'The bookies will be open in London Colney at 10.30.'

So we would cycle off down the drive from the training ground and turn left as though we were heading off for a bike ride. But we'd wait five minutes until the coast was clear and then head for London Colney, have three or four bets and just sit there.

'How can you just sit there and not have a bet?' Merse would say. He was in another zone. He would then put £50 on some bet or other, but he was shit at it. The bookies would be full of Tiddlywinks, Paddies and smokers, but he loved the place. After about an hour, I'd say, 'We've got to get back. They're not stupid – they'll suss us.'

One day it was raining and there were puddles everywhere, so we had to splash water and mud over us to make it look as though we'd been riding through the countryside.

I don't know whether that break in Marbella did us much good, because after we came back we played Manchester United in the Rumbelows Cup and lost 6–2 – the club's worst defeat in 40 years and our biggest home defeat of the century! Up until then, we had only conceded seven goals in 17 league and Cup games, but that game Lee Sharpe scored the only hat-trick of his career. We were 3–0 down at half-time and even got it back to 3–2 at one stage. We thought George would go spare, but he came in the dressing room and said, 'Superb second half, freak result.' Then he gave us the next day off. He didn't want to be seen to panic and he had also seen that none of us had jacked it in.

The next game was against Liverpool, a massive match as they were top of the table even though we were still unbeaten in the league. 'I am going to play the same team again,' said the Boss, 'apart from one change. Grovesy, I'm going to play David O'Leary as a sweeper.' I didn't like being dropped, but we won 3–0, their first defeat of the season, so he was right.

That was a bad start to the month for me, but it was nowhere near as bad as the December Tony Adams had. He began it on the

8th by being sent off at Luton for the first time in his career, then on the 19th he was sent down for four months for reckless driving. In May, he'd been three times over the drink-drive limit after an accident in his Sierra XR4.

The first we'd known about the accident was while we were waiting at Heathrow to go to Singapore for our end-of-season tournament the previous summer and we were all wondering where Rodders was – we reckoned he'd overslept. We were all in the departure lounge when he came through in his club blazer with his tie all skew-whiff. There was a big kerfuffle with Rodders and George and Gary Lewin, and then they all started hitting the phones.

'All right, Rip Van Winkle?' we said, but he said he'd just gone through the windscreen of his car. Now Rodders loved a Jackanory but, as he said that, he shook his head and all this glass started coming out of his hair. Some of it fell on my hand.

He told us he'd gone to a barbecue on the Sunday afternoon, and then went through some traffic lights on red, so he turned round to look behind him and hit a telegraph pole, and all the electricity in the street went out. After that, he hit a garden wall and went along the street before ending up in someone's garden. The Old Bill had breathalysed him and then let him go, so he did well to get to the airport really, but he had no kit and no luggage.

We got on board the plane and said, 'Fancy a sherbet, Rodders?' and of course he had one. We didn't realise just how bad the accident was or what a fuss it all caused till we got off in Singapore and found out it was all over the papers in London. His motor was a right mess.

Of course, he shouldn't have been drinking and driving, but if he had been done in the summer he would not have got sent down. But the timing was all wrong. He took so long to get his defence and the references on his behalf together that he ended up front of Southend Crown Court just six days before Christmas. They were looking to make an example of someone and he was perfect.

The players' Christmas 'do' was on the 19th, the day he was due in court. We all met up at 11am at Highbury as Paul Davis had sorted somewhere for us all to go out near the ground. A couple of the girls who worked in the office came in crying, and then Bouldie said, 'Have you heard? He's been sent down.'

'Yep, very funny,' I said. 'Is it seven days for wearing dodgy gear?'

'No,' they said, 'it's for four months.'

I had never known anyone who had been sent down before. For a while, we thought perhaps we shouldn't have our 'do', but after ten minutes we decided to go ahead with it. 'It's what he would have wanted,' I said. Then we decided to go to a bar near Pentonville Prison because we thought he might be in there. We all had one for Rodders as we looked out of the windows at the prison wall. He would have liked that.

We knew he would get through it all, though. He was strong like that. We all wanted to see him but he was only allowed a limited number of visits. Gary Lewin went to see him about his fitness, and most of the lads wrote letters. I asked if there was any chance of his car-park pass and match tickets, as he wouldn't be using them for a while. He used to wear Val Doonican cardigans, so I added, 'At least you will have some decent clothes for a while.' Yes, Rodders had had better months.

As for the Boss, it was us against the world again. He called another meeting, and Andy Linighan filled in for Tony and played brilliantly in a 0–0 draw at Villa Park. After that we didn't lose a game until February when we lost 2–1 at Chelsea, and that was only because Steve Bould got injured. It was the only game we lost in the league all season.

25

Rodders came out of Chelmsford Prison in February and it had changed him. You could tell that he was different somehow. Meanwhile, I'd picked up an ankle injury and Kevin Campbell had started to emerge as a first-team player, so I didn't get involved properly until around March. I would have 10 or 20 minutes here and there as a sub, but that was about it. But we had gone ahead of Liverpool by April and the league title looked like it would be between us and them, and I reckoned I would have enough appearances to collect a medal if we won it.

April was also Lewis's first birthday and we had a party one Sunday to celebrate. We had a bouncy castle for the kids – and a big barrel of Kronenberg 1664 and another of bitter for the grown-ups. It turned into a real session and when I went into training on the Monday I must have stank. I felt groggy too and just wanted to get through the day. We had a match the next day but I probably wasn't going to play.

Then the Boss said, 'I'm going to make one change – Grovesy, you're playing.' Oops. I had no co-ordination and I felt terrible, and even on the Tuesday on the way down to Southampton on the coach I still had the shivers and the shakes – the DTs, in other words. We checked into a hotel before the game and I said to Merse, 'I'm struggling here. I don't think I'll last half an hour.'

Eventually, we got to the ground and I still felt like death, but I thought, Fuck it, I'll play. Once the game started, I felt all right – the adrenaline must have kicked in – and we ending up drawing 1–1. That was the only time I ever played with a hangover for the Gooners, and it was all by accident – I didn't think I'd get a game. I certainly don't recommend it.

By mid-April, we were going strong for the Double and faced Spurs in the Cup semi-final. There was no neutral London ground big enough to take all the 78,000 fans, and it was the first time a semi-final had been played at Wembley.

Gazza and Gary Lineker scored for them but then Smudge pulled one back for us just before half-time. I was sub and the Boss then sent me on with about a quarter of an hour to go with his usual instructions: 'Go on and run around.' As soon as I got on the pitch, though, David Seaman let one from Gary Lineker through his hands and that's how the score stayed: 3–1. You don't want to lose a semi-final to anyone – but to lose to them makes it ten times worse. We saw ourselves as normal working-class kids, and that Spurs side somehow seemed to come across as the flash bastards up the road.

When we got into the dressing room there was David Seaman crying. Poor 'H' was beside himself. Gazza was famous by then for crying, but that was because he thought he was going to miss the World Cup Final. It got to 'H' because he reckoned he had let the team down, but we all knew he hadn't. To see this hulking great Yorkshireman sat there crying his eyes out was very strange. I can understand people feeling high when they win, but I have never understood how they could be so low in defeat. Of course, you feel disappointed, but this... Merse and I got in the big bath at Wembley and were pissing ourselves – we thought it was funny to see 'H' blubbing.

But that was the Double out of the question, so there was just the league left. With five games remaining, it was between us and Liverpool. In the run-up to these final games, the club took us all away to a posh New Forest hotel, the Meon Valley Country Club, for a midweek break. Paul Davis had a testimonial golf day organised at South Herts Golf Club, but we couldn't be bothered to play and by the time we got on the coach to go to the New Forest, a lot of us were pissed. David Hillier got a bit lippy so Rodders gave him a slap, as you do, but that was one of the rare times there was any trouble like that between players. It was only a slight slap anyway – there were never any big punch-ups.

On the Thursday, we went to Fontwell Races and the Gaffer let us take the coach. I think we all gave Merse about £50 or £60 each and formed a syndicate to have a bet with and, of course, it had all gone in about an hour. We had to be back at the hotel for dinner at 7pm and by the time we turned up the ten of us who'd gone were all pissed.

I was sitting down for dinner in the hotel restaurant when all of a sudden I smelled burning. I couldn't make out where it was coming from, but I could certainly smell something. Then I realised what it was – it was my flesh. Nigel Winterburn, who was sitting next to me, had taken a spoon and warmed it over a candle flame. Then, when it was red-hot, he'd put it on my bare arm. I must say I thought it was funny at the time too, but when I woke up in bed the next day the sheet was sticking to my arm where he'd put the spoon and I was in agony. I still have the scar to this day.

One night during this trip, Warren Aspinall, who was playing for Portsmouth at the time, came into the hotel bar and was lording it a bit. 'Flash twat!' said Merse and the next thing I knew he was saying, 'I've got a fire extinguisher.' Sure enough, he'd got the hotel fire extinguisher off the wall and was holding it. I said to him, 'You haven't got the bollocks,' and he said, 'I have.'

Someone must have told Aspinall, though, because he left, but then our coach Stewart Houston walked into the bar. Merse pointed the hose at him and said, 'Don't move – I've got you covered.'

'Put it down,' said Stewart.

'One more step and I'll blast you!'

We all said to Stewart, 'You can't let him talk to you like that!'

Then, of course, Merse let him have it – and the rest of us and the bar staff too.

It was a break to remember too for our defender Colin Pates. He was fast asleep in the reception area at about 1am when Anders Limpar came up to us with a handful of little stones he'd taken from the flowerpots around the foyer. He looked at Colin and said he was going to put them in his foreskin! Then he went over to Patesy, carefully undid his trousers and delicately placed the tiny stones around his foreskin. Then we left him. He had to be woken up by the girl receptionist to go to bed.

The next morning, Bouldie came down and said, 'I wouldn't want to be the one who did that. If he finds out, he will rip their head off!'

When Patesy came down I said, 'It wasn't me!' and we pointed out that, whoever did it, it wasn't personal.

'Not personal, putting stones in my foreskin? I'm woken up by a hotel receptionist with my trousers round my ankles and stones in my foreskin. Not fucking personal?!!'

Anders was quiet for the rest of the day, but he did say, 'I don't think Colin is very happy.' No one bubbled him. He was a lucky man.

One day, Anders came into the changing room at London Colney, stripped off and it was like looking at an alien. He'd shaved off all his body hair, including his pubic hair. He said he and his wife had been messing around and she had shaved all his hair off. 'It will make me go quicker,' he said. We didn't say anything – he was Swedish, after all.

Anders had come to us from Italy and when he first arrived he was furious as he thought Arsenal were underpaying him. He had agreed his terms, but when he got his wages he thought there wasn't enough money. He hadn't realised that in England your wages are always 'gross' – before tax and other stoppages. He thought the amount agreed would be what he'd be getting in his pocket, not the 'net' figure. We had to explain it to him and he wasn't very happy.

After playing football in Italy, he couldn't believe the amount of drinking we did. He would say, 'Imagine how fit you all would be if you did not drink.'

I still think that going out with your mates helps, though. What's the point of all that success if you can't enjoy it? I've always thought it's bollocks about not getting carried away with success. Go for it, because you don't have too many chances to celebrate success in life.

I could have celebrated something around that time – an international cap, would you believe? Jack Charlton was in charge of the Eire team and Niall Quinn was a regular in it. A lot of Englishmen with Irish parents or grandparents were being chosen, so I would say to Quinnie, 'I could play for Ireland – I had an Irish red setter as a kid.'

I mentioned this to my dad and he said that my granddad on my mother's side came from County Cork. So I told this to Theo Foley, who also worked with the Irish side, and he said, 'I'll put your name forward.'

A little while later, after a match at Highbury, Theo said, 'Big Jack is here – go and have a word. Quinnie, why not introduce him?'

So we went into the old players' lounge and there in the corner was Big Jack enjoying the Arsenal hospitality: 'Jack, here's Perry Groves,' Quinnie said. 'Grovesy can play for the Republic.'

'Oh, can he?' said Jack. 'There's an Ireland B on Tuesday night – you can play up front with David Kelly.'

I said, 'All right – thanks, Jack,' but I was thinking, 'Will he remember?'

'Great,' Quinnie said afterwards, 'you can fly over with me.'

'I can't just turn up out of the blue,' I said. 'He might have forgotten.'

I said I needed something official, but Theo said, 'No, it's not like that.'

'I can't fly over,' I said. 'He might say, "Who are you?" when I get there. If they want me, they can make contact with the club.'

I said to my dad later that, if it had been the full squad, then fair enough, but it wasn't worth it for the B squad. So that was the end of my international career. It was all or nothing – and it was nothing.

Come the start of May, we were top of the table and the only team that could catch us was Liverpool. We were playing at Sunderland on the Saturday and the game was put back until 5pm for live television. As we travelled up there on the Friday, I felt really bad with gastric flu. I went to see the Boss on the Saturday morning and told him I was struggling.

'No, I want you to play,' he said.

It might have been May but it was a typical Wearside day – rain, wind, everything. It was horrible and I played the whole game, which ended as a 0–0 draw. Afterwards, I weighed myself and found I'd lost 9lb during the day from being ill and then playing. The Boss said, 'Well done.' We all stayed at the Noke on the Saturday night then I went straight home and slept all through Sunday to recover and felt better after that.

On the following day – a Bank Holiday Monday – we were playing Manchester United at home and Liverpool were playing Nottingham Forest. Liverpool had to beat Forest to even have a chance of the title, but they lost 2–1 before we'd even kicked off so the Championship was ours for the second time in three years. There was a party atmosphere at Highbury that day – and George dropped me, the bastard.

I wasn't even the sub – it just showed how ruthless he could be. If I had been sub, I would still have been all right, but this... I was going to go straight home, but decided to stay. I'm not saying that United didn't try, but let's just say they seemed to be in the party spirit too. We beat them 3–1, with Smudge getting a hat-trick.

Afterwards, as everyone was celebrating on the pitch, George said to me, 'Grovesy, get out there. You are part of this too,' but I said, 'Bollocks! You're having a laugh, aren't you?' He just walked away. I went out in my suit, but it wasn't the same. There aren't too many times you can play against Manchester United and enjoy it, are there?

George then gave us time off until the Friday and took us to a restaurant in Cockfosters to celebrate. He was paying, so I made sure that I caned him on that.

The final game of the season was against Coventry City at home and I was named sub. We beat them easily and I got on towards the end and touched the ball twice – once when one of their players smashed it right in my face and once when I scored to make it 6–1. I felt I'd earned that medal – I'd been involved in 32 out of 38 league games.

The players had booked a table at Langans restaurant that evening, and throughout the night Rodders and his then girlfriend Jane would go from one table to another and sing Cher's 'Shoop Shoop Song'. It was all right to begin with, but as they did it every half-hour we'd all had enough by the end of the night.

The next day, it was the open-top bus again and I had 200,000 supporters eating out of my hand as we drove through Islington. I was on the Town Hall balcony – as I had been two years earlier – and I gave them my usual 'Ooh To Be a Gooner', 'My Old Man Said Be a Tottenham Fan' and 'We Are the Champions'. Even though I'm tone-deaf, the crowd loved it. As I said, milk any success that comes your way, because there are more than enough downs in a career.

26

When we reported back for training for the 1991–92 season, English teams were back in Europe, which meant we would be in the European Cup. But the Boss hadn't made any new signings. A year earlier, he had brought in David Seaman, Andy Linighan and Anders Limpar, and I thought it was a mistake not to do something in time for the new season. David Hillier had come in and done well, but I still thought the Boss should have signed another midfield player.

At the beginning of August, the Makita Tournament was played at Highbury between us, West Ham, Sampdoria of Italy and the Greek side Panathinaikos. This was the first time the crowd really started to boo me. There had been mutterings before, but then I would play well and the moaners would go away. This was different.

We had beaten the Greeks 1–0 and were playing Sampdoria the next day in the final. I came on for the last ten minutes and the reception I got was frosty to say the least. The game ended 1–1 so it went to a penalty shoot-out to decide who'd win the trophy. Now it's funny, but when penalties come around even the top players go missing, and four or five of our players didn't make eye contact with George. 'Grovesy,' he said, 'do you want to take one?' and I said, 'Sure.' There were 30,000–40,000 people there, but it wasn't the European Cup, after all. I'd taken one before in front of 60,000, at a tournament game in Singapore when I scored past Bruce Grobbelaar.

Paul Davis missed his penalty and as I came forward I could hear these groans and people saying, 'Oh no, not him.' But I put the ball on the spot, and then ran up to take the kick. As you do this, your heart rate increases and your legs don't feel like normal, and if the crowd are groaning that doesn't help either!

The good news was that I sent the goalkeeper the wrong way. The bad news was I also put the ball past the post. We lost. None of the lads had a go at me and I was pleased that at least I'd had the arsehole to take the penalty. If there's a challenge, I'll go for it.

Then Anders came up to me after the game and said, 'A bit of advice, a word. Maybe next time you should try chipping the ball.'

I said, 'Say that again.'

He said, 'Chip, chip – try chipping the ball.'

I said, 'You cheeky Swedish twat! You've got the front to stand in front of me and tell me how to take a penalty when you didn't have the bollocks to take one yourself!' He was the fans' favourite at the time, so for good measure I added, 'You could take a dump in the centre circle and they'd still love you and sing your name.'

In fairness to him, he came up to me at training after that and said he was sorry. He had been only trying to help and he hadn't realised what he'd done.

For the first couple of games, I was sub, but I could see that cracks were beginning to appear. We had only lost one game in the league the previous season, but now we'd lost two of the first four. We even managed to lose 2–1 at home to Coventry City when Lee Dixon scored the best own goal I have ever seen in my life. He'd got some new boots and they were rock hard – he should have worn the boxes they came in rather than the boots. Whatever they were paying him to wear them, it wasn't enough. In the first minute, he just took one touch of the ball and chipped it superbly over David Seaman. He must have got a five-iron out of his bag, not a wedge. I sat on the bench and just started laughing – it was so funny.

My first start of the season was wide on the right at Crystal Palace. We beat them 4–1 and I was back to something like I should be, but I still got dropped. I know it's hard to believe, but I don't think Arsenal ever lost a game that I actually started in.

Then we played Austria Vienna in the first European Cup game at Highbury for 20 years and beat them 6–1. They were like an Austrian pub side really. Smudge got four and Anders got one too.

On the following Saturday, the stuntman returned. Anders was suspended so I played against Sheffield United. We beat them 5–2 and I scored with a great right-foot volley – even George said it was fantastic – and made two others. I thought, Thank fuck for that, but then I had to go off injured after 50 minutes. I didn't realise it then, but that was the start of my real Achilles problems.

After that, George bought Ian Wright from Crystal Palace for £2.5 million and I knew that meant I would be pushed further down the list of forwards. Wrighty was an out-and-out goalscorer – I didn't think he fitted in with the way George wanted his forwards to play, but what he brought to the club was loads and loads of goals. He made his debut at Leicester in a Rumbelows Cup match and I was on the wing. He did bugger all for 44 minutes and then scored a great goal, the kind only he could score.

When Wrighty first came to the club, we didn't get on at all. In training, most of the players would get slaughtered at one time or another and in the five-a-sides the worst player was given a yellow bib. If he did something wrong, I'd call out, 'How much did he cost?' and I could hear him muttering, 'You'd better shut up.'

After training, I had a bath and went under the water. As I came up, there was Wrighty, standing alongside the bath in his training kit. 'Enough,' he said. 'Me and you outside – now!'

'It's a bit chilly out there,' I said.

'Now!'

'Go and get your brothers! Grow up, Wrighty. Have a word with yourself.'

Then I got out of the bath and thought that, if he had gone for me, it would have been like the nude wrestling scene in *Women in Love* with Oliver Reed and Alan Bates.

It didn't bother me at all, but at Palace Wright and Mark Bright had been the big stars, and I don't think he was used to taking it from a squad player like me. But after a couple of weeks I think he began to realise that everyone at Arsenal got it at one time or another and he began to get used to it. He started handing it out himself and we got on all right after that.

Of course, he went on to be one of the great players in Arsenal's history – a fantastic goalscorer, and the fans loved him for it. I've seen him at a few dos since, and once, after I hadn't seen him for three years or so, he immediately asked, 'How are you? How are Lewis and Drew?' For him to remember my lads' names was great. Top man.

But, as I said, when he joined us, it meant I was going further down the list. For Wrighty's league debut at Southampton George took a squad of 16 and I was the 17th! I travelled down with the rest of the players, but it was taking the piss really, and Wrighty capped it by scoring a hat-trick.

I knew I was on the way out and then we played Leicester in the Rumbelows Cup replay at Highbury. I got on for the last ten minutes or so of the game and there was a large chorus of boos as I came on the pitch. I was playing up front and, as I got there, the Leicester player Nicky Platnauer turned to me and said, 'Fuck me, your fans hate you more than our fans hate me!' There's always someone worse off than you, isn't there? At least I'd made him feel good about his situation!

If you have a crowd of 35,000 at a game, it only takes 1,000 to groan or boo at the same time and it's a lot of noise. One or two thousand disgruntled supporters can make a massive difference. If a player says that it doesn't affect him, he's a liar. If it's away fans who are doing it, then it means that you are doing your job, but, if it's your own fans at home, that's different. You try harder, but you get more tense. It puts pressure on you.

Tony Adams or David Rocastle could have had four or five poor games and no one would get at them, but by this time it only took one bad pass and that was it for me. I don't know where it came from or how it started, but it never happened with the fans who followed us away from home. We would take 4,000–5,000 fans to away matches and they never got at me. It was different at Highbury, though, and I think it was mainly the lower East Stand who decided to have a go at me. It didn't make me hide, but you end up not playing with as much freedom as you should – it's a subconscious thing.

Arsenal had had kicking boxes before – Graham Rix and Paul

Davis had both been through it – but that was the worst time for me. I wasn't depressed and I just hoped that I would be able to play my way through it. But the new signings meant I wasn't getting the chance to even get on the pitch. I was training with the reserves and, as a first-team squad member training with them, sometimes it was hard to motivate yourself.

The reserves' trainer was George 'Geordie' Armstrong, a real Arsenal legend, a member of the Double-winning side and a great guy. The younger players, though, weren't giving him the respect he deserved – they didn't realise that he had played 700 games for the club. One day, one of them, Paul Dickov, said to him, 'Fuck off, you don't know what you're talking about.' He was an upstart Jock midget, all 5ft 6in of him, and he was a lookalike for Ali Campbell from the band UB40. And he'd done fuck all in the game.

'You little twat,' I said, 'go and apologise.' Geordie wasn't making a big issue of it, but I was. But Dickov had 'little man syndrome' and he told me to fuck off. I said, 'Say that again and I will rip your fucking head off.' He just turned around and walked away mumbling. A little while later, I'd calmed down and said to Dickov, 'Do yourself a favour and apologise to him in private.' He did.

There was another funny incident when I was training with the reserves. One of Geordie's favourite training exercises involved the German Game, dividing the players into three teams of eight. Two of the teams would play each other in one half of the pitch, and if the defending team could dribble the ball over the halfway line they would take on the third team. That way you would rotate the three teams so that two were playing and one was having a rest.

We were the attacking team at one stage and there just didn't seem to be anyone to pass to. I said to Geordie, 'Are you sure we've got eight?' and he said yes. It still looked to me as though we were a man short when I heard Geordie saying, 'What the fuck is he doing?'

We all turned round and looked at the penalty area in the distance. There, all by himself, was Andy Linighan – standing on his head. All the lads started pissing themselves and Geordie said to him, 'What are you doing?'

Andy, who had a dry sense of humour, just stopped standing on his head and gave us his famous John Wayne walk back to the halfway line and said, 'Sorry, Geordie lad. I just had to get it out of my system.' He was pissed off training with the reserves too and it was his way of making some sort of protest – but it was still funny.

But I trained with the first team too, so I wasn't put out to grass, and on 23 October 1991, we played Benfica – managed by a certain Sven-Goran Eriksson – in their 120,000-capacity Stadium of Light in Lisbon. I came on for the last 15 minutes and we got a good 1–1 draw thanks to a goal from Kevin Campbell.

For the return at Highbury, I was on the bench. We went ahead through Colin Pates and even though they equalised I thought we were hammering them but couldn't finish them off. I came on for the last ten minutes but it was still all square at the end, so extra-time was needed. We went for it, but they did us on the break and we lost 3–1.

Next day, the papers took us apart, saying English football was behind the continentals, but George took it well. I thought it was just naivety on our part – we'd been sucked in by them. I enjoyed the game, even though we'd lost, and at least the crowd didn't get at me that night.

Earlier in October, the Boss had bought Jimmy Carter, a winger, from Liverpool for £500,000. I was actually pleased, because it meant he was a squad player and I would be on my way soon. I hadn't tried anything clever with George – if I had, I wouldn't be training with the reserves, I'd be grazing with the cows in the fields nearby. But with Jimmy there in the squad all I had to do was sit tight and someone would come in for me and I'd get a move. I was 26, 27 and these were the best years of my career. I was in love with Arsenal, but Arsenal weren't in love with me any more.

But Jimmy messed it all up by having a nightmare. He was a good player and a great lad, but he just couldn't settle, and George and the rest sussed that I was more effective than he was. I'd even say to Jimmy, 'Liven up!' in training just to gee him up. It didn't do much good.

In mid-November, we played Oldham away and were 1–0 down when I came on as sub. They had a left-back called Andy Barlow – although he played like Ken Barlow – and he kept threatening to break my legs. I was laughing and telling him he had some front. If it was someone like Stuart Pearce saying that to me – not that it was his style – I'd have been bothered, but not this muppet.

In the 86th minute, I nutmegged 'Ken' and crossed for Ian Wright to head the equaliser. As we were trotting back, I shouldered Barlow and said, 'Oops.' Then we had a bit of a niggle and David Rocastle came over to sort things out, but I told Rocky it was all right and said to Barlow, 'You try and break my legs and I'll try to put it through yours.' So he spent the last five minutes trying to break my legs, and I spent the last five minutes trying not to get my legs broken.

The first week in January, we played at Wrexham in the Third Round of the FA Cup. We were the current Division One Champions and they had finished 92nd in the league the previous year, and they were still around that position. I knew that if I played I would be Cup-tied and that would reduce my chances of getting a good move. So I feigned an injury and said my back was playing up. That was the first time I'd ever done that, but George sussed it and Gary Lewin said, 'George wants you to travel.'

I was sub and at half-time we were 1–0 up and playing well. I came on and we were still in front with just seven minutes left when we gave away a free-kick on the edge of the box, so I went back and took my place at the end of the wall. They had a 37-year-old midfield player called Mickey Thomas – who used to play for Manchester United – and he ran up and took the free-kick. He really smashed it and as I jumped up I turned my head to look and thought, That's got a chance. A nano-second later, the ball was in the net: 1–1.

A couple of minutes later there was a scramble in our area and they managed to score. There were only about five minutes left and I thought, This ain't good. We ended up losing 2–1 and it was the biggest upset in the Cup for 20 years. They still talk about it up in North Wales, presumably because there isn't much else to talk about. It didn't bring Mickey Thomas much luck, though. He was arrested a few weeks later on counterfeiting charges and ended up being jailed for 18 months for passing forged banknotes to YTS players.

After the match, George said to us, 'Get yourselves ready for a backlash – you're the ones who lost it. Don't talk to anyone.' He expected us to get turned over by the papers because of the result, and he was right again.

You wouldn't think things could get much worse, but they did. As the coach headed back to London, Gary Lewin came up to me and said, 'The Gaffer wants a word with you.'

I went up to where he was sitting at the front of the coach and he said, 'Grovesy, sit here.' That had never happened before. 'I think we have a problem, don't you? I've been told there is a bird who has gone to the papers and said that you and another player were shagging her and a mate on New Year's Eve.'

What had happened was that my long-time girlfriend Jenny had come to see me in the hotel in the West End where we were staying the night before our game with Wimbledon on New Year's Day. I'd got a note from her saying she was downstairs in the bar and when I went down she had a mate with her. You can guess what happened next, and to cut a long story short someone had gone to the papers with the story.

I sussed that the Boss had just heard about it and he was trying to find out more. It would be a serious breach of club discipline and I would be fined and everything. I said to him, 'I don't know what you're talking about. If this bird is in the papers, I'll sue her.' Then I went to the back of the coach and told the other player involved what had happened. He was in a terrible state, but I just said, 'Look, we can't do anything about it. If she says I was just "pump-pump-squirt" that would be terrible. I want her to say that at least I was a good shag – there would be some kudos there.'

As soon as we got off the coach, I phoned Jenny and she told me that a woman we both knew had tipped off the newspapers and they had been on to her. She said she had been offered £10,000 to talk about what went on, but she'd turned them down. Next morning, I rushed out yet again to buy the Sunday papers – but there was nothing in them. Saved again, good girl.

I wouldn't say I was depressed around this time – that's not my style anyway – but life was not as it had been. I just told myself that I was still playing for Arsenal and I was still earning a good living. Something was bound to happen.

27

Towards the end of the 1991–92 season, we played at Notts County. It was a horrible place to go but we ended up winning 1–0 and I played well, so I thought I might get something out of the season after all.

We were playing Norwich at home next and I was with the rest of the lads at the Noke Hotel for our pre-match meeting. The Boss read out the team and I wasn't in it. Then he said he would name the subs at the ground. As soon as I heard that, my head went. Even the other players couldn't believe it, and I said I was going to see him. Normally, the protocol is that, if you have a problem, you go and see the Boss after a game. Merse said, 'Don't do it,' but I went to see him after the team meeting.

'What's the matter?' he asked.

'Fuck off,' I said. 'You know what the matter is.'

'We'll talk about it later.'

'No, now.'

Then he said, 'You were excellent on Saturday, but I want to play differently at home. The crowd have been getting on at you at home and you've handled it all right, but I am not sure it mightn't affect the rest of the team.'

'Because you have a few nuggets in the crowd, you won't play me at home?'

'No – perhaps it's just for this game.'

Whether or not it was an excuse I don't know, but it was the last thing I wanted to hear. What it meant, as far as I was concerned, was that now I probably wouldn't even be considered for home games. I would end up playing all the crap games away from home where you have to scrap for everything, but none of the matches at Highbury where we would be attacking a lot more of the time.

I'm not going to name names here, but I've known of players who went to George and asked not to play because the crowd were having a go. I wasn't going to be like that – if there was a problem I'd face it head on. The only good thing was that the crowd started having a go at Jimmy Carter too, so they weren't having as big a go at me.

By now, it was the middle of March and the next game was against West Ham at Upton Park. I was playing wide on the right against Julian Dicks and, although he snarled and kicked, I didn't mind because he couldn't run. The problem was that every time I got the ball he battered me. He battered me 13 times so I said to the referee Brian Hall, 'This is embarrassing. This is GBH!'

In the second half I thought, I'll have to get him sent off here, and after 55 minutes he eventually booked Dicks. But he kept battering me again and again, and in the end I thought, If the ref ain't going to do anything about it, I am. So I gave Dicks the same as I gave Graham Roberts, a tackle from behind, and he squared up to me. That was my first tackle and I got booked. I couldn't believe it, and a moment later Dicks battered me again.

So I said to the referee, 'Are you going to do something about this?'

'If I send him off, there'll be a riot,' he said.

I said, 'That ain't my problem.'

And then he said, and I swear this is true, 'Why don't you swap wings? Just for ten minutes – it'll defuse the situation.'

Five minutes later, we were winning 2–0 – Wrighty had got two goals. Dicks was still battering me and George could see that by now I had the hump, so he took me off.

Their fans weren't happy. They were deep in relegation trouble and they came on the pitch three times during the game. The police had to get them off using Alsatians, and they even let two of the dogs off their leads. One of the dogs lost it and jumped over the wall, all ferocious and snarling, into the crowd. It disappeared and 30 seconds later it was thrown back on the pitch whimpering. Someone had bitten one of its ears off! Don't mess with the Hammers.

As for Julian Dicks, he was quite good on the ball, but I was too quick for him. He's a good lad, actually – he was just a lunatic on the pitch.

I didn't play in the next match but then I was in the side to play Wimbledon, who were playing at Selhurst Park at the time. It wasn't a nice place to go – the pitch was always crap and there was no atmosphere.

After about 20 minutes, the ball bounced between me and their Danny DeVito lookalike, Terry Phelan. I knew I had to go for it and I knew he was going to do me. He came in late and got me with his elbow, cracking two of my ribs. I couldn't breathe and had to crawl off the pitch like a dying fly. That was the season over for me. Finito. My second and third ribs were broken so that was me out of action for six weeks, and I missed the rest of the season. Leeds won the title and we came fourth.

Meanwhile, my mate Roy McDonough had taken charge of Colchester. They were in the semi-final of the FA Trophy and I became their unofficial mascot. They played Macclesfield in the second leg of the semi and I went up to watch on the supporters' coach. Colchester won – they went on to win the Trophy that year – and they said I might as well stay over that night and celebrate with them.

My ribs were mending and I was having a drink with the players back at the hotel – they had some heavy drinkers there, good pros – when I noticed some of the administrative staff in the corner and I said to Roy, 'Have a look – your fan club.' They were all smiles to Roy's face but they were less than complimentary about him behind his back.

They were sitting in the corner, behind some little wooden railings, at a table that had lots of drinks and glasses on it. I took a run from the bar, tucked my ribs in, went over the railings and executed a commando roll on their table, scattering everything. 'That's enough of the soccer chat,' I told them.

When I got back to the bar, Roy just said, 'I see your ribs are getting better.'

In fact, my life was getting better as, on 21 May 1992, my second son Drew was born at the same Colchester maternity hospital as his brother. This time, I didn't mind if it was a boy or a girl, but when I saw that it was another boy I was overjoyed; I had the same overwhelming feeling as at Lewis's birth. Then we realised that we hadn't chosen any boy's names. I said to Mandy, 'I like Drew,' which was Lewis's middle name but we didn't use it. So 'Drew Daniel Groves' it was.

When we went back for training for the 1992–93 season, I knew I was on my way out, so I was determined to get fit in case someone came in for me. But after a week I had a soreness in my Achilles tendon, so I saw one of the club's doctors, Dr Leonard

Sash. It turned out the sheath around my tendon was thickening and the two were rubbing together. He decided to give me a cortisone injection to help reduce the swelling.

I hoped it wasn't like another injection I'd had earlier from the other club doctor, Dr John Crane, who was also the England doctor. I'd been kicked between the balls and my arse by a goalkeeper and a great big swelling came up. Dr Crane said he had never seen anything like it before and showed it to two students who were with him and even took pictures of it before he injected me. It was like *Readers' Wives*!

Anyway, Dr Sash gave me my injection and it was eye-wateringly painful as he had to wiggle the needle about, but it did clear the problem up. The problem was now that I had missed two weeks' training and, if you do that at the start of the season, then you're playing catch-up. I was in the reserves but I knew I wasn't fit enough. Then we had some injuries before a game at Blackburn and the Boss asked me how my Achilles was. I told him it was a lot better, and he said that he might need me to travel with the team.

I was nowhere near match fit, but I came on for about 15–20 minutes and I surprised myself. I'd put thoughts of a transfer out of my mind because of my lack of fitness, but, a couple of days later, Gary Lewin said to me, 'The Boss wants to see you.' I wondered what it was about, but, when I walked in, George said to me, 'I've accepted an offer of £750,000 from Southampton for you.' My first thought was, Fucking hell, that's a lot of money. Alan Shearer had just been sold and he only cost £3 million. 'It's up to you,' George added, 'but they want to see you today.'

It was his way of saying they didn't need me any more, but he said it in a nice way. He even said that if I couldn't sort things out over the deal with Southampton I'd be welcome back. Then he said, 'You've won your medals, now go and earn your money.'

I was unshaven and as I walked out he called out, 'Oi, you could have had a shave!'

'I didn't know you were going to get rid of me,' I replied and he just laughed.

My financial adviser John Hazell was away so I took Jerome Anderson with me. I don't like agents – I think they're an unnecessary evil in the game – but I liked Jerome, who looked after David Seaman, and I trusted him. As Jerome drove me down, I was quite excited about the move, because it was obvious that I had no future at Arsenal. No matter what they say, players do think about the transfer fees they cost – I just wished mine could have been £1 million.

I then met the Southampton manager, Ian Branfoot, who said he wanted to play me as a winger on either side. He wanted someone with pace and energy, and he'd seen me play at Leicester and liked the way I tracked back too. He liked my work ethic. I told him I didn't think I was match fit, which seemed to surprise him a bit. I mentioned the Achilles but he just said, 'Medical will sort that out.'

The package they were offering worked out at about £100,000 a year and, as I was on about £75,000 at Arsenal, it meant a pay rise. Southampton wanted me to sign a four-year contract and I wanted two, so we settled on three. I made a mistake there – I should have signed for four. My advice to any footballers signing a deal is to make it for as long as possible for the security it brings.

Another piece of advice is to take two or three days to think over any move. I agreed on the spot with Southampton and I should have thought about it a bit longer. If a club really wants you, they'll hold on for a little while. I would have been better off waiting and getting myself fit – another club would have come in for me. It was all just too quick. Suddenly, I was no longer a Gooner.

28

Ian Branfoot had got £3 million for Alan Shearer and, with it, he signed me, Kerry Dixon from Chelsea and David Speedie from Blackburn. It looked like he'd got a great deal, but it turned out to be the biggest waste of money in their history. I got injured, Kerry Dixon had a bad back and David Speedie just wanted a bit of confrontation. But he also bought Ken Monkou from Chelsea, so at least he got his money's worth with one player.

On the drive back from signing, Jerome Anderson asked me if I was happy with the deal and I said yes. I reckoned it probably made me one of Southampton's highest-paid players and hoped to have a regular place in the side. Most important, though, it gave me some security at 27, especially as Drew had been born that summer.

In football, we have a thing called 'empty-peg syndrome'. You can get changed next to the same guy for five years and then you go in one day and the peg where he hung his clothes is empty. Not long before I moved, I remembered going to the ground one day and seeing the Boss in a car with David Rocastle. Everyone was quiet and they told me that the Gaffer had accepted an offer from Leeds for him. Rocky was crying his eyes out. It broke his heart. He was a great player but he had started having knee trouble the year before and I guess George and the medical staff reckoned they'd had the best out of him. He was the nicest man in the world but he was never the same player at Leeds or Chelsea – he just didn't have the same feeling for those clubs as he did for Arsenal. I thought, If the Boss is prepared to sell *him*...

By the time I got back to the ground, it was all locked up – I couldn't even pick up my boots. I thought, I've been coming here practically every day for six years and now that's that. Ian Branfoot had given me Saturday off so I drove back to Colchester and went out with my mates Chinney, Big Nose and Ginge. I got the champagne out – why not? When I did pick my boots up, all the players and staff wished me good luck and George said, 'You're welcome back any time.' Then I drove off into the sunset – never look back.

Southampton's training ground at Marchwood was all right, but it wasn't as good as London Colney. I had a hard running session on the Monday and played for the reserves on the Tuesday and scored a good goal. Everyone is looking at you in your first game so as I walked off I thought it had gone well. Then Ray Graydon, who was in charge of the reserves, said, 'Perry, you've got to do some running.' I thought, Fuck off, but it seemed the Boss wanted me to get fit. I had to go in on the Wednesday even though the others didn't, and on the Thursday Ian Branfoot told me, 'I'll play you on Saturday.'

'Fine,' I said, 'but I'm not match fit.'

He said, 'You did all right the other day.'

Not quite the same though.

Kerry Dixon, who hadn't been scoring since he was signed, asked me how I'd got on in the reserves, so I said we'd won and I'd scored. 'At least we've someone who can score,' Kerry said.

Matt Le Tissier was a god down there and, with him, me, Dixon and Speedie, the side looked great on paper – but on grass it didn't work!

We played Middlesbrough at home on the Saturday and I came off injured after about 70 minutes so they sent a lad called Nicky Banger on. We were 1–0 down and we ended up winning 2–1 and everyone was happy. But the atmosphere wasn't the same as at Arsenal – there was none of the camaraderie. No one was unwelcoming, but there were three factions: the youngsters, the older players and the new signings like me.

I don't suppose I endeared myself in the sense that when you arrive you should work your way in, but, my character being what it is, I was loud and taking the piss and mucking about. But, if a player likes a laugh and a joke, it can be perceived as, Who does he think he is?

One example at Southampton was a trip we had to Marbella, a bonding exercise. We were meeting at Gatwick and meant to turn up in club tracksuits, but we'd played the day before at Ipswich and after the game I had gone back to Colchester. I couldn't be arsed to go all the way to Southampton to pick up my tracksuit, so I wore one of my own, a lime-green number. I also turned up wearing a pink-and-black Foreign Legion hat and, when they asked me why, I explained, 'It's because I'm a ginga and it keeps the sun off.'

During the trip, a few of us went to a bar in Puerto Banus and were having a drink outside. Terry Hurlock – who ended up being a close mate; he had a dry sense of humour – was showing us his Rolex watch which he called his 'Mercedes 190E' and said, 'That's a proper kettle.'

I asked to look at it and reckoned it was a moody – a fake – and went to throw it in the port. Just as I pulled my arm back, Tim Flowers jumped over and grabbed me and said, 'No! It is a real one.' Tel had had a big transfer to Glasgow Rangers a while earlier and had bought himself a £10,000 Rolex out of it – and I was about to throw it in the water! After that, whenever anyone reckoned that it was a moody I would get him to put it in a pint to show it was real.

We went back to the Attalla Park Hotel at about 9pm and the worst group I have ever heard was playing. I thought, This needs livening up, so I told the lads I would dance on stage. They said, 'No, you won't,' so I took five forward rolls down the aisle, one forward roll on to the stage and then knocked the mike stand over as I started dancing. A Brit abroad! The manager was watching and obviously thinking, For fuck's sake – what have I bought here? And then the hotel manager asked me to leave the stage.

The lads put me to bed and when I woke up the next morning I thought they'd all gone home without me. The room was empty and none of my gear was in it. I went out into the corridor and saw a couple of the lads, and told them I couldn't remember much about the night before. They said that I hadn't known my room number so they'd just put me in an empty bed and left me.

Ian Branfoot sent Lew Chatterley, his assistant, to talk to me. 'It wasn't good last night, was it?' he said. 'You are trying too hard to fit in. Be yourself.'

'Lew,' I said, 'I *am* being myself!'

He just looked at me. There was nothing he could say.

During the trip, Matt Le Tissier and a group were playing cards in the hotel and he asked me if I wanted to play. I said, 'No, I don't play cards.'

He said, 'You can be sub like you're used to.' I saw it as locking horns, as a putdown.

'See you, you lazy, big-nosed twat,' I said. 'At least I had the bollocks to be playing for Arsenal. If I had your talent, I wouldn't be playing here. You want to be a big fish in a little pond, staying where you are.' I wasn't having a go at his talent – he was fabulous, one of the most gifted players I have ever seen – but it's horses for courses. He could have farted at Southampton and he would get a standing ovation. He never tested himself.

The lack of preparation at Southampton surprised me. We worked three or four times harder at Arsenal. You'd think it would be the other way round: with lesser players you would want to put more work in. Of course, we worked on set-pieces and the like, but it was nowhere near as detailed as at Arsenal.

One example is that on the coach with Arsenal we would have water to drink, but Matt Le Tissier would sit there with Coca-Cola and a Mars Bar. At Arsenal, we would stay in a hotel on the Friday night before a game and we would have fish or pasta. The Southampton lads would be queuing at the carvery. Tiss would have big slices of beef and four or five Yorkshire puddings, and he wasn't the only one.

Having said all that, my first goal for Southampton – against Leeds – was when Tiss hit a great diagonal ball inside Tony Dorigo – who was Stuart Pearce's stuntman in the England team – and I smashed it past John Lukic. I would have liked to have played more with Tiss, because he was a great player.

I scored my second goal for Southampton at home against Wimbledon – a great, dipping volley. But I also went in for a challenge with Vinnie Jones and I kicked the bottom of his foot and did my right big toe. When I took the boot off, the toe was all swollen. On Monday, it was agony and there were shooting pains. I went to see the physio Don Taylor and he put some ultrasound on it.

I said, 'There's something wrong here.' I told him I was struggling and couldn't put my boot on, so he said they would put cortisone in it.

I was injected before the next game against Crystal Palace but I could feel a shooting pain every time I kicked the ball. They gave me another dose at half-time and by the time I got back on the pitch my whole right foot was numb – I couldn't feel a thing. I had no touch and with 10 to 15 minutes to go they took me off. The physio said that even if it was broken the treatment was the same, which was true, but I wanted to know.

So I went to Southampton General Hospital and waited for one and a half hours in the outpatients' department for an x-ray. Imagine Thierry Henry doing that. Nowadays, players have an x-ray for dirty fingernails!

Eventually, the doctor came in and said, 'Mr Groves, you have a very interesting fracture.' It turned out I had a 'half-moon' fracture of the toe. 'You haven't played for a while, have you?' he asked.

'I played last night.'

'Well, you're out for four to five weeks with this,' he said. 'I suppose you are in some pain?'

'Yes!' I said.

So I didn't play for a few weeks, then made a couple of appearances as sub. Then one January night we played Middlesbrough away and, while I was warming up, my right calf muscle felt as though it had a knot in it. I sat in a bath of hot water to try to stretch it off. By this time, I reckoned some of the other players must be thinking I was always moaning about being injured.

We kicked off and after about 30 seconds I laid off a header and went to turn to make a run. I felt a whack and reckoned their full-back Jimmy Phillips had booted me, but he hadn't. Don Taylor came on and I told him the full-back had booted me in the calf. I limped off and tried to run it off along the touchline in front of all these Teessiders but I had to say, 'Don, there is something wrong with my calf. I can't put any weight on it.'

So I had to come off and I was lying in the bath when I heard this clump, clump of studs coming down the corridor and then Terry Hurlock came in. He'd been sent off for fighting. He got in the bath and he said, 'Bloodnut' – that's what he called me because of my red hair – 'what the fuck's happening here?'

I took some painkillers and put a tubi-grip put around my calf. I knew something was not right – I was even having to go upstairs sideways. Back at Southampton, Don gave me some treatment on my calf.

On the Friday, I went on the bike in the gym, but when I got there I couldn't even get my right foot in the stirrup, it wouldn't fit. It was flopping around and the other players were all laughing.

I got changed and went to see the manager and told him, 'I can't walk, I can't put my foot down. I'm telling you now, I've no chance of playing on Saturday.'

He said, 'Thanks.'

The club doctor, Dr Chris Lawrence, came in on the Monday for his surgery and I reported to him. Again, I said, 'There's something not right here.' I lay on the bench and the doctor put his fingers on my Achilles and said, 'Don, he has a problem with his Achilles.'

I went to Chalybeate Hospital in Southampton and they found

that there was a 90 per cent tear in my Achilles – it was hanging by a thread.

They operated on me the next day and I was told I would be in plaster for six weeks. I'd always thought it was a waste of time to be injured and be a non-drinker, so at least I could have a drink. Still, when you have a serious injury like that, you always worry whether it means your career is going to be over. I learned how to drive my automatic car with my left foot and after four or five days I'd got used to it. I tried to keep my weight down and would try to do some sit-ups, but that was all.

The club said they'd pay six months' rent on a house for me, but then they increased it to 12 months. I knew that would be me finished for that season and I'd have to go in to get fit in the summer, but I didn't mind that.

The plaster would be changed every two weeks, and after six weeks they took it off for good. I looked at my chicken leg, but I was happy because it looked as though everything had gone fine. I was given some non-weight-bearing crutches, so I wouldn't put weight on my leg, and I started to walk around gingerly – obviously.

Mandy and I still had the house in Colchester and one Friday we drove back there from Southampton with the boys in the back of the car. When we got there, Mandy got out with all the bags and I came behind with the boys and some clothes thrown over my shoulder. I got to the front door and hopped up on my good left leg. But it caught the doorstep and I instinctively put my right foot down and there was a massive bang – an actual noise. It was the tendon snapping.

The pain was unbelievable – I had tears in my eyes and I was seriously sweating. I couldn't move for half an hour. At the back of my mind, I knew something serious was up, but I still went out in Colchester that night! Later, a rumour went around Southampton that I had fallen over pissed, but it wasn't true. I can't remember the number of times I'd been to nightclubs and fallen over and not hurt myself, but this was at home and I hadn't had a drink. That will teach me to try to help my missus.

On the Monday, they took me to the specialist who said he would operate next day to try to reattach it. I asked if I would play again and he said it was a 90 per cent tear followed by a complete rupture. 'It's not looking good,' he said. I was operated on at the same hospital and told I'd be in plaster for eight to ten weeks. Suddenly, it dawned on me that my career could be over at 28.

29

In January 1994, Ian Branfoot resigned and a new management team came in. Alan Ball, the 1966 England World Cup player, was put in charge of the players and Lawrie McMenemy was made general manager.

When I came out of plaster the second time, I had no movement in my ankle at all, and even after a while it still had 30 per cent less movement than my left. I even had a general anaesthetic while they tried to manipulate the joint to give me more movement, but it didn't work. So I went to Lilleshall in Shropshire for rehab – a place players hate. The resources are great and so are the staff, but they work you really hard. I had my own room there and stayed from Monday through to Friday, before heading home on Friday afternoon. I swam a lot, went on a bike in the gym and used the rowing machines. I had to learn to walk again really, as I just didn't have the confidence.

There were lots of sportsmen there and during my time the

footballers included Vinnie Jones, Neil Sullivan, Ally McCoist, Trevor Steven, Gary Stevens and Alvin Martin. The jockey Richard Guest was there too and he gave us some wonderful tips.

Sometimes, we'd go to the pub, and one night, after we'd had six or seven pints, Vinnie was driving me and Neil back in his white BMW. It was pitch black and he'd got some music on when he suddenly went, 'Shshh, shshh.' Now Vinnie is a nice bloke but he's as mad as a bucket of frogs. He stopped the car, turned to us and said, 'Can you hear that?'

'What?' I asked.

'It's a fox,' he said. 'I can hear it.' Then he opened the car door and started doing a fox's mating call, just like animal impressionist Percy Edwards. Next, he started walking around the car making this call – I was in tears watching him. Then he opened the boot and got out a shotgun! For a good ten minutes, he was walking up and down the road with his gun, looking for the fox. Eventually, he got back in the car. 'They kill chickens,' he said. 'I'll get him tomorrow night.'

I got on really well with Vinnie. One Friday afternoon as we were all getting ready to drive home I saw I had a flat tyre. I was on crutches and that meant I'd have to wait for an AA man to come and change it. Vinnie, who'd often helped me in the canteen, just took his jacket off and changed it for me. Top man.

I was only meant to go to Lilleshall for two weeks, but I ended up being there for five. We weren't supposed to enjoy it, but at Arsenal we'd had the Tuesday Club so now at Lilleshall we had the Thursday Club. I'd hire a minibus and we'd all go to Cascades nightclub in Telford, 12 or 15 of us. It's amazing what a few Stellas and a bit of Abba will do for you. But all the time I was thinking, Am I finished? One day, it would be all right, the next I'd be lower than a snake's belly. Back at Southampton, I'd be in training, but I still couldn't run properly. It was like having a pebble in my shoe.

To relax after training, Terry Hurlock would sometimes say to me, 'Fancy a quick light ale, Bloodnut?' and we'd go out drinking all day till about 9pm. But at weekends he'd say. 'Fancy a proper drink?' and we'd go up to London. I'd often end up ringing an Indian restaurant in Southampton to get them to deliver a takeaway that I was supposed to take home to Mandy. We were living at Chandlers Ford near Southampton by then – Mandy liked it there, and we'd made friends with our neighbours Adrian and Sarah too.

When Ball and McMenemy took over, I was training and running, but I knew I was nowhere near right. They kept asking me, but I was miles away from being fit. I told them I was a senior pro – meaning I knew whether I was fit or not – and I wasn't ready. But two or three months later they played me in the reserves and it was embarrassing. I came off at half-time and I really had the hump. They were trying to prove a point, but it wasn't fair on the other lads – they were having to carry me.

Laurie McMenemy came up to me the next day and I told him, 'I told you I wasn't ready. You made me look like a twat.'

'We wanted to see what you could do,' he said. 'Anyway, the manager wants to see you.'

So I went to his office and Ball said, 'I saw you play last night and I have to say you looked like you were struggling.'

I said, 'Are you taking the piss? I told you I wasn't ready, I wasn't fit. I've been out for 14 months. What do you expect?'

Then he said, 'Perhaps you want to think about other things?'

What he meant was doing something different from football. Perhaps the club thought that I was insured for £500,000 and, if I quit because of injury, Southampton would get that money. If I played somewhere else, though, they wouldn't get a penny. He was trying to say to me, 'We're trying to do you a favour.'

After that, if he said good morning to me, I'd look out of the window to see if it was day or night. His ideas as a coach were good, but I didn't think much of him as a man. I didn't want to feel like that about a World Cup winner, but his man-management was pants.

I decided to get fit in time for the next season, and when it came I played a few games in the reserves. I was a better player in some ways, but I had lost a yard and a half of pace and it had been my pace that had made me different before.

Then, one day, near the start of the 1994–95 season, McMenemy said he wanted to loan me to Swansea and I said no. Why would I want to go there? Then he mentioned a month at Wolves, and I said no again.

But I'd got fit, though I realised I would never be as quick again, and I was back in the first-team squad for a pre-season game at Orient. It was good to be back again, and halfway through the second half they put me on... at left-back! That capped it for me. They weren't going to give me a chance at all. I could see what was coming. If they had sat me down and talked about it like men, that would have been OK. I was 29, not a kid.

Eventually, I was offered £75,000 to buy out my contract. If I'd been a single bloke, I'd have played for two or three years in the lower divisions. But I couldn't have got a long-term contract as I wouldn't have passed a medical for the insurance, so it would just have been a month-to-month contract and that would have been jeopardising Mandy and the boys' future.

So they came back with another offer of £100,000, but that included six months of my contract. McMenemy was on about how they were doing this out of the goodness of their hearts, but that was bollocks because if I didn't retire they got nothing at all. In the end, we reached a deal where I got £150,000 and about three or four months' wages, but it was on condition that I retired.

I'd also been paying into a pension throughout my career, and as a sportsman I could access it at 35. In those days, if you could retire from football and your house was paid for, you'd done OK. Well, I had a four-bedroomed house all paid for and, although football was finished, I wasn't feeling sorry for myself. I had a good wife, great kids and a lovely home. How bad could it be?

30

After my earlier affair with Jenny, you'd think that I would have learned my lesson. But soon afterwards I was at it again. My football career was coming to an end, and we had a helper – not live-in, thank goodness – who looked after Lewis and Drew back in Colchester.

We had a thing for about a year until her mum and dad found out and, shall we say, weren't best pleased. Her dad wanted to rip my head off – still does, come to that. So I took all the blame and her parents said to me, 'We won't tell Mandy if you knock it on the head,' and I said, 'OK.' Mind you, I managed to give it another month before it all ended. So that was that. If only...

A year later, I was 'cold calling' for a soft-drinks company when I got a tax demand for £10,000 that the Revenue reckoned, wrongly, that I owed them from Southampton. I'd just finished reading that and was thinking things couldn't get much worse when the phone rang. It was Mandy's brother on the line.

'Have you got something to tell Mandy?'

Oh dear – he'd heard through family links of what I'd been up to with the nanny. I blustered for a while and said, 'It's finished, it's old news and the one who will get hurt most is Mandy.' It was all true, but he insisted either I told her or he would. So I put the phone down and told her what I'd done. I had no choice.

She asked me how many others and I told her none.

But she kept on asking so I said, 'Not many,' and a little while later that had become 'a few'. There was then a silence and I said, 'Shall I get my coat?'

'Yes,' she said.

I hadn't just betrayed her this time, but her family too. They are really close and I'd managed to hurt them all, and this was unforgivable. So I moved in with my old Colchester pal Steve Whitton for a while and Mandy let me see the boys, even though I had been an arsehole. Lousy husband, good father.

After two or three months, I came back home and that seemed to be that. But it wasn't. It was around this time, while I was still on Southampton's books and sorting out the end of my career, that I started going out at weekends. For years I hadn't been able to, as we normally played on Saturdays, so Fridays were out of bounds, but, like me, Steve Whitton and Roy McDonough were coming to the end of their playing careers. We were like kids who'd just discovered a sweet shop: Friday was the best night to go out.

We'd normally start at Trotters wine bar in Colchester, which would be packed by 5.30pm. Most people had just finished work for the week and were unwinding. They might stay for an hour or so before going home to get ready to go out somewhere else. The place would thin out for a while and then around 9pm the later crowd would come in to spend the rest of the night there.

Me, Steve and Roy did a double shift – we just stayed put all night! Soon we were going out Friday, Saturday and Sunday – and the more you go out the more opportunity there is to play.

There was a place in Colchester called the Cellar Bar and we'd go there on Sundays. We'd have lunch with our wives and get pissed, and then the three of us would head off without them to the Cellar Bar. The wives thought we would just be going out drinking: I don't think it crossed their minds what we really got up to. The Cellar Bar was the only good place open and there would be a live band playing, so the place would be packed and there'd be loads of girls there.

Now Roy was a very good cricketer and he knew a girl there who had been out with one of the local players. They started talking and as the night went on it became clear that he had a chance. I was busy sniffing around her mate but she wasn't having it. Then Roy said he was off with the girl he was talking to. 'Grovesy', he said, 'I'm going – do you want to tag along?' Did I? I was there like a little Jack Russell – he couldn't shake me off. Back at her place, she started to strip, and Roy started to strip – so I joined in. Afterwards, we left in a taxi and the driver could tell that we'd had a really good time – he said, 'What have you two lads been up to?'

The next Sunday, we were back at the Cellar Bar and the girl was there again. This time she had brought a mate of hers over, and she was pretty fit too. It didn't take long until Roy and I realised what was going on and I was like a little Jack Russell all over again. The four of us left together and went back to the flat, and all four of us had a play. Again, we left in a taxi and it was the same driver as the previous week. He turned to us and said, 'Whatever it is you two are on, can you get me some too?'

The end with Mandy eventually came after I went into Trotters wine bar and spotted a really attractive blonde, just my type. We got talking and I found out her name was Judith Manning, and after a while the key question cropped up – was I married? Quick as a flash I said I was estranged – isn't that a great word? – and we carried on chatting. She gave me a lift home and as we neared our house I told her to drop me round the corner. Of course, she asked why, and I replied, 'My mum is looking after the kids and she wouldn't like to see me arriving home with another woman. You know what they're like.' In fact, Mandy was at home with the boys, so it would have been suicide.

You don't need to be a genius to work out where this all led: Judith and I started to see each other. I was trying to keep both women on the go at the same time, but, as I've said, Colchester is like a village and it's hard to keep something like that quiet. The main hope is that, because they're all it, no one will split on you. But it had to come out, didn't it?

One night, I went out with Mandy and some other couples for a drink at our local. The trouble was, the landlady was the girlfriend of Judith's former partner, and she was aware of what was going on between the two of us. So one night about midnight – during one of the lock-ins we often had – I went to the toilet happy as could be, but when I came back everyone was sitting there as grim as death – and there was no sign of Mandy.

One of the lads in the group said to me, 'I think we have a problem.'

'What's that?' I said.

'Mandy's just been told you're shagging Judith.'

Oh dear – here we go again.

Mandy was in the other bar in a terrible state when I went to see her and obviously I denied it. I said I didn't know anyone called Judith and so on and so forth. But the seed had been sown and eventually Mandy found out – you can't keep a secret in Colchester. The dialogue was pretty much the same.

'Shall I get my coat?'

'Yes.'

This time I got my own place and, whenever I went round to see the boys, Mandy was civil to me. For four or five months, it was in-out, in-out – not an ideal marriage. When I moved back in for spells, I would want to be with Judith, and so it went on.

Matters came to a head when I went to a Colchester home game where Steve Whitton was assistant manager. The club had a deal where you could have a meal and as much as you could drink for £10 before a game. Well, we well and truly hammered that I can tell you – talk about drinking a profit! They later put it up to £25 but I'd still come out ahead. Anyway, as the boozy evening wore on, I asked another pal, Ray Mayze, what I should do. I was torn between Mandy and Judith.

Ray and his wife Christine were friends of Mandy's and mine and he said, 'Who would you rather be with tonight?'

I said, 'I would rather be with Judith.' I thought about it for a moment and turned to Ray and added, 'Thanks. I'll tell Mandy now.'

'Don't tell her now,' considerate Ray added quickly. 'It'll ruin the night.'

But I told her that night, stressing that I'd never desert the boys. What a reaction that provoked. She promptly packed all my stuff in eight black plastic bin bags, put them in the boot of our car and drove around to Judith's. I wasn't looking forward to it, but she marched straight up to Judith's front door and pressed the bell. Judith answered and Mandy told her, 'I have a delivery for you. Good luck.' Then off she went, leaving me and all I possessed in eight bin bags.

The next day I was driving around in my car and I still had all the plastic bags in the back. I went to Lexden tennis club and, just to rub it in, someone said, 'Hello, Perry. Off to the tip?'

'The tip?' I said. 'That is ET in there – Emotional Turmoil. My life is in there.'

But I don't blame Mandy for one second. She couldn't keep getting hurt and upset. Together, we sat the boys down and told them what was happening. Then we went to the school to make sure they knew about the divorce, and asked them to keep an eye on the boys to see there was no reaction.

I gave her the house that was all paid up – that was £100,000 worth in the mid-1990s – plus some other money, and I happily paid maintenance for the boys, so at least we had a 'nice' divorce. We get on well now, and always go to the lads' sporting events together.

Judith and I have now been together about nine years in total... sort of. We've actually split up on five or six occasions during those years and I've had liaisons with other ladies in between, but not at the same time as I've been with Judith – honest. But Judith often points out that, on the day Mandy dumped me at her door as a delivery, she didn't sign for me, so our relationship doesn't count. Let me think about that...

31

My last game as a professional was for Southampton reserves at Norwich in 1994. I was sorting out all the financial side of leaving the club and, although Mandy knew about it, no one else did. As it was at Norwich, all my family came to see me play. I doubt if there was even 100 people watching the game, and half of them must have been my family. I was up front and it turned out to be the best I'd played for six months. I wasn't as quick as before, but I was sharp and I was enjoying myself. We were 2–0 up and I was thinking, Am I doing the right thing here?

They had a young centre-forward called Ade Akinbiyi and he was playing poorly. He ended up being transferred in a few million-pound moves. During the first half, he said to me, 'You has-been, you're finished. I'm on my way up.' His first touch was pants so I said, 'Fuck me, you can trap it further than I can kick it.' At least my tongue was as good as ever.

Then there was a clash of heads between me and one of their

players and I had to go off and have some stitches. When I came out again, the reserve-team manager, a big Geordie called Dave Merrington, told me they'd put the sub on. I said, 'Are you winding me up?' Talk about an ignominious end to my career. 'What you've done to me is a disgrace – you are out of order. A bit of respect would have been all right,' and went off and had a shower. In fairness to him, he did later say sorry – he had been worried about his young team being a man short.

I was still fuming in the bar afterwards and that was where I told the rest of my family that I was calling it a day. As I was talking to them, there was a tap on my shoulder and there was Ade Akinbiyi and he said, 'You – outside now.'

I looked at him and said, 'Look, silly bollocks, I don't need this at the moment. Fuck off.' I thought, Here we go, but just then my dad, Big Ginge, stepped in and grabbed hold of his hand. 'I'll give you one piece of advice,' he said. 'Don't lay hands on my boy.'

I pulled my dad away and someone grabbed silly bollocks. It wasn't the way I'd wanted my career to end: stitches, subbed, a row with the manager, and one of the other team having a go. Still, never a dull moment.

Twelve years on from all those matches for Colchester reserves in the backwaters of East Anglia with people trying to eat me during games, here I was in a tiny ground getting in punch-ups after the game. The wheel had come full circle.

So that was it with Southampton, but it's only right that I mention of couple of the players down there. For a while I stayed with Peter 'Quifford' Whiston at his flat in Ocean Village, then I stayed with David Hughes, who also did some DJing for about three months. He had some interesting characters come round from time to time, I can tell you. It's at times like that that you know who your mates are.

The insurance deal with Southampton meant that I couldn't play full-time professional football again, but I still managed a few games after that. I was enjoying my Fridays and Saturdays off, to tell the truth, and I wasn't missing football at all. But my mate Roy McDonough was playing for Dagenham and Redbridge in the Conference and said their manager, Dave Cusack, was interested in me playing for them. It involved training on a Tuesday and playing on a Saturday and £275 in my hand, which I thought would be money for the weekend.

The gates were about 300–400 and there were no full-time pros, so for a lot of the players football was their second job. But they wouldn't be helped – they looked at me as though I was talking through my arse. They had chips on their shoulders and one of the reasons they couldn't play at a higher level was they couldn't handle the pressure.

I played three or four games and then we played Altrincham at home. I got lumped about five or six times in the first 15 minutes so I said to the referee, 'Are you going to do something about it?' But he just said, 'Get on with it.'

This big lump kept clattering me and I asked the referee again to do something about it but he didn't. So, two or three minutes later, the ball bounced and I went in with my Eric Cantona two-footer around the guy's neck and shoulder. We both went down in a cloud of dust like wildebeest – and I got sent off.

I was sitting in the dressing room thinking, What am I doing here? when Roy – who's been sent off 21 times in his career – came in. He'd been sent off too and we both looked at each other.

So I was thinking of jacking it in and then Dave Cusack dropped me. I asked him what that was about and he said, 'You're playing too much football.'

'See your money?' I said. 'Stick it up your arse.'

I couldn't stand the cheating there, the lack of ambition in their players. They should have expressed themselves, but they were happy drifting along. They should have been enjoying themselves, not hiding.

After that, I played for Canvey Island, who I think were in the Ryman League Division Two at the time, or as I called it the Dog and Duck League Division 28. It started off all right and we won my first game 2–0, but then in another game at 2–2 I was pulled off by their manager, Jeff King. I had been substituted enough times in my career not to be upset about it, but I couldn't stand that he couldn't see that the players were cheating on him. By that, I mean not getting into positions to receive the ball, not helping their teammates out.

'I thought you looked tired,' he said, so I told him, 'You're an embarrassment. Stick it up your arse.' It was a shame, because I got on well with him to begin with and found him quite a decent character, but I wasn't impressed with his football knowledge. The story got put around that it was because I was too fat, but it wasn't true.

In 1996, Mandy and I were divorced. I had given her the house, so when an old friend of mine, Ray Mayze, who had a business selling fruit-flavoured-water franchises, asked me to help him out in his warehouse I agreed. It got me out of the house and it stopped me going on the piss.

It went so well that he asked me to go out on the road cold-calling, selling to gyms, cafes and newsagents. I said yes, but I told Ray I was not working Mondays as I would be recovering from the weekend and I wouldn't work on Fridays either, because I'd be getting ready for the weekend. I was self-employed so that was fine.

I had my pension at 35 but, of course, I needed to work and

Raymondo taught me a lot after the cosseted life of a professional footballer. I worked for him and his various franchise companies and I'm eternally grateful for the money and the life-lessons he gave. I even had to learn how to go on holiday – the organisation, tickets, passports and so on had always been done for me by the clubs I was at or by Mandy.

I was working in Sandbach in Cheshire when a friend of Ray's called me. He had known Francis Lee, the former England and Manchester City player, for 30 years and Frannie owned a company called PermaPlay, a playground-marking company who were looking for someone to help them to expand in the south. The PFA had sent some former players for interviews but they hadn't got a background in sales. I told Ray about the interview and he said to go and have a look.

I was told there was an interview at 11am the next day, which was at Holmes Chapel. I said that I was just down the road at Sandbach, so it wasn't a problem. What was a problem was that I was driving an old-ish Citroen AX and hadn't got any decent clothes with me. My old mate Peter 'Quifford' Whiston lived in the area so I borrowed his wife's car and his jacket, trousers and shirt.

Despite wearing Quifford's gear, I was offered the job and, after finishing off my commitments to Ray, I started work there in March 2004. I design and sell playground markings for infant and primary schools. They're a great company to work for and I have job satisfaction because I see how playgrounds are improved and how kids enjoy their sport and general activities.

After I left Arsenal, the club, as always, was never out of the headlines. Merse admitted his cocaine, drinking and gambling problems. Rodders too said he was an alcoholic, and even the Gaffer, George Graham, left after the revelations of his 'unsolicited gifts' in some transfers – the bung scandal. In my opinion there is too much of a counselling culture with today's footballers. Merse and Rodders were binge drinkers, not alcoholics. The two reasons are: nobody could play at that level and be an alcoholic and secondly, if they were alcoholics, then I was!

I got in a bit of trouble myself in the year 2000 that it would be wrong to hide. I'd been drinking in Colchester with pals and must have got through 16 or 17 bottles of Budweiser. I went back home to meet a girl I was seeing, but she didn't show, so foolishly I got in my car to drive back to the centre of Colchester. I was driving in the direction of the police station when all of a sudden there were flashing lights and sirens and I was pulled over. I suppose the fact I was in a gold Daimler Sovereign with private – not personalised – numbers plates made me stand out. I hadn't drunk for an hour and felt all right, but I was breathalysed and I was about three-and-a-half times over the limit.

At the station, I demanded to see my brief, and when the police asked who that was I said, 'I haven't got one.' An hour later, I demanded a phone call, and when the police asked who I wanted to call I said, 'Don't know.' I was just being a pest.

When I was released in the morning, they had to breathalyse me to make sure I was OK to drive, but I was still two-and-a-half times over the limit. So I set off walking and I had never felt so low. I felt I'd let Lewis and Drew down. Then a policeman I knew pulled up and he offered me a lift. I asked him if he was taking the piss but he told me, 'Half the station have been waiting to get you for something for ten years. The other half would have taken you home.'

I was banned for 28 months, fined about £200 and ordered to do 130 hours' community service. I also had to go to an alcohol-awareness course where you keep a diary of your alcohol intake.

We were told the average safe intake for a man should be 28 units and for a woman 21, but everyone lies, of course. My intake for the first week was 45 units and I said that was below average for me. But I know I will never get done for drink-driving again. If I'm drinking, I won't drive.

Even those meetings had their funny moments. There was a young builder there, a really fit young guy, who said he had got through 88 units that week, and then added, 'To be honest, I haven't been on it much this week.' He said if he had five pints of Stella – which was three units a pint – he would class that as not having a drink. Normally, he said, Monday through Thursday he would have six or seven pints a night, and Friday and Saturday 10 to 15 pints each night.

The lecturer told the bloke, 'you've got a problem and you must do something about it. What have you decided to do?'

He just said, 'I'm never going to drive again.'

My community service was at the Barnardo's shop in Colchester. First, I was in the shop, cleaning and collecting, but after a while I was promoted to work in the books section. It was there one Saturday that I heard on the radio that Rocky, David Rocastle, had died. He was just 33 and had had cancer. I went numb. It took my breath away and I welled up. It was the first time that anyone I knew who was young had died. Everyone will go on about his talent, and quite right too, but he was also a genuinely nice person. There is a saying that only the good die young and it's entirely appropriate for Rocky.

32

Arsenal have had some great players in their time: Charlie George, Ian Wright, Tony Adams, Dennis Bergkamp, Thierry Henry – I could go on and on. So, when it comes to listing the most talented, the bravest and most successful men ever to pull on a Gunners' shirt, you would hardly expect my name to be among them. And it isn't.

When I left the club, and later finished with professional football, I reckoned I'd be remembered by a few but forgotten by most, the same as most guys who earned their living that way. The occasional Arsenal devotee would recall my efforts on their behalf, or someone in a pub might ask, 'Hey, didn't you play for...?' and then try and remember which team it was. Then the odd know-it-all might chip in by telling me, 'I never thought you were any good in the first place.' All the usual stuff really.

But it's not as simple as that. Something strange happened. Somehow I became a cult. Yes, I did say cult. Over a decade after

I last played in the red-and-white strip in a competitive game, Gooners fans still chant my name at games. They sing songs with my name in it. I'm interviewed for football magazines and, thanks to the internet, there are websites about my life and my career.

So, how did it happen? Well, during my days with the club I had a love–hate relationship with the fans. Some of them loved to hate me, but a lot recognised me for what I am, a Gooner through and through. They also realised that, even if I wasn't the best player ever to pull on a pair of boots in the cause, I would still give everything, and I mean everything, for the 90 minutes I was on the field – or however long the Gaffer decided it should be.

I also think my game had a special link for the fans on the terraces or in the stands. I wasn't out of this world. I didn't have talents that were way above anything they could ever dream of. It was as though I was one of them and had ended up playing for the team we'd all dreamed of playing for. And when they saw me have a bad day at the office (and there were a few) the distance between me and them probably didn't seem very big at all!

Plus, when you are a ginga, you do tend to stand out in a crowd. The red-haired players who make it to the top are few and far between, so, with all those normal-coloured barnets out on the pitch, I stuck out like a beacon. I suppose the fact that I shaved my hair down either side and at the back and had a little gelled tuft at the top, making me a double for the cartoon character Tintin, made me a little easier to spot. But I liked it that way.

So, during my Highbury days I expected to get the bird quicker than most players if things weren't going too well. What I didn't expect was that one day as I was playing I'd hear a version of The Beatles' 'Yellow Submarine' wafting towards me.

With its sing-a-long tune and shout-a-long chorus – ideal for drunks or soccer fans – the song was perfect for a parody, and who better to use to take the piss than yours truly? So I heard thousands of voices singing the familiar chorus with 'We all live in a Perry Groves world' substituted for Lennon and McCartney's original words.

That was bad enough, but then it came to the verse: 'At number 1, it's Perry Groves / At number 2, it's Perry Groves / At number 3, it's Perry Groves...' I could run through it all if you like, but I'm sure you've got the idea by now. And it ends with a line that sums up my career: 'At number 12, it's Perry Groves...'

Then it was back to 'We all live in a Perry Groves world, a Perry Groves world, a Perry Groves world...' Catchy, isn't it? In recent years, Arsenal have sent out a team without one British, let alone English, player in the line-up. I often wonder what that collection of highly paid French, Dutch, German, Brazilian and the rest must think as they hear this 40-year-old tune being sung about a player they've never heard of.

If ever you want to check on the lyrics, not that they need much checking, just log on to some of the websites that are about me. They have names like PerryGrovesWorld and WeLovePerry. Before you can ask, the answer is no, I didn't set them up myself – I wouldn't know how to. I didn't pay anyone to do it for me, either, and I don't know who's behind it all, although I did get an email from one of them asking me to be a guest at their wedding. I would have gone too, but I was away.

Come to that, I don't understand much of what is on these sites, but I know they are funny. In between a handful of real facts and figures, there's a world that looks as if it was created by Spike Milligan – on one of his bad days. Recurring themes are my hair, my likeness to the pop band Bros, the way I wore the short shorts of the day pulled up fairly high, and the Anfield match where we achieved Mission Impossible.

There's loads more jokes too, involving the Queen, the Orange phone network, Lucozade and the like, and the chants they urge fans to yell at the millionaires who run out for today's Gooners: 'Two Tintins, there's only two Tintins...' and 'Perry for England!' They even launched a campaign to get me in the current England side – they obviously know their stuff – on the basis that my legendary long throw-ins might bring a new dimension to the national team! There's even practical advice on how to achieve the hairstyle I wore, involving – so they tell you – glue, candle wax, flour and treacle and lots of other ingredients.

When I go to charity events or supporters' evenings, fans are always approaching me to say that all this is done in good spirit – they're having a laugh WITH me, not AT me. The fans know that if I hadn't played for the Gooners I'd have been watching alongside them. Some guys wouldn't know whether to be flattered or insulted by all this. Me, I'm flattered. I just think it's all a good laugh. No one gets hurt and, if it makes people smile, fair enough.

I've always taken what I do very seriously, especially the football, and I wouldn't like it if anyone says otherwise. But I've never taken myself too seriously. I like reading about myself in the newspaper or seeing myself on the football pitch on TV, and what's wrong with that? Any player who says they don't is lying. But I never let it go to my head. I never believed my own write-ups, as some guys do. I never got a false view of my own importance. I was brought up too sensibly by my parents to ever fall into that trap, and for that I'm grateful.

I know what is important, and that's my sons. In May 2005, I took Lewis and Drew to see Arsenal play Manchester United in the FA Cup Final in Cardiff. The Gooners won 5–4 on penalties, but before the match we were walking to the Millennium Stadium when the most bizarre thing happened: a group of five 'Perry Groves' came towards us. By that, I mean five men who were all wearing masks with my face on in glowing orange and ginger colours. It was my picture from my playing days and these guys had had masks made from them. This, remember, is almost 20 years after I first signed for the club, and well over a decade after I stopped playing.

What my boys must have thought, God only knows, but they just pointed and pissed themselves laughing. I could have gone up to the bunch, but thought better of it. My Tintin haircut has long gone and I've put on a pound or two, so they didn't recognise me and we passed each other without a word.

Epilogue

I still play occasionally for an Arsenal Celebrity XI with former players and people like the singer Tony Hadley and the actors Ralf Little and Phil Daniels. I've achieved more in my life than I dreamed of, but my greatest achievement, together with Mandy, is having two fantastic boys. Watching Lewis and Drew play sport gives me more pleasure than when I was playing, even though they have gone over to the Dark Side to play rugby. They're excellent cricketers too.

It can't be easy for them having me as a dad, because I'm ultra-demanding. It's 'do as I say, not do as I do'. I'm not perfect, but I can show them the pitfalls of life, and I'm there if they need me, no matter what. Every parent sees their children through rose-tinted spectacles, but they've developed into pleasant, affable young men. And I must mention too the lady in my life, Judith Manning and her lovely daughter Kate, who is the same age as Drew. They are both very dear to me.

I enjoy life and my glass has always been half-full, not half-empty. People wonder if I am bitter that injury ended my career, but I never was. My Achilles could have snapped when I was 16, not when I was 28. As it is, I've somehow become a cult and if they ever decide to make a film of my life I've already worked out the title: *Perry Groves: 1,001 Greatest Throw-ins.*

People can say anything they want about me – I don't mind – but when I die the reports will say: 'Ex-Arsenal Player Perry Groves Died Today.' That will do for me.